X.400 and SMTP
Battle of the E-mail Protocols

X.400 and SMTP
Battle of the E-mail Protocols

by John Rhoton

Digital Press
Boston • Oxford • Johannesburg • Melbourne • New Delhi • Singapore

Digital Press™ is an imprint of Butterworth–Heinemann.

Recognizing the importance of preserving what has been written, Butterworth–Heinemann prints its books on acid-free paper whenever possible.

Butterworth–Heinemann supports the efforts of American Forests and the Global ReLeaf program in its campaign for the betterment of trees, forests, and our environment.

Library of Congress Cataloging-in-Publication Data

Rhoton, John.
X.400 and SMTP : battle of the E-Mail protocols / by John Rhoton.
p. cm.
Includes bibliographical references and index.
ISBN 1–55558–165–X (alk. paper)
1. Electronic mail system—Standards. 2. Computer network protocols. I. Title.
TK5105.73.R47 1997
004.692—dc21 97–14875
CIP

British Library Cataloguing-in-Publication Data

A catalogue record for this book is available from the British Library.

The publisher offers special discounts on bulk orders of this book.
For information, please contact:
Manager of Special Sales
Butterworth–Heinemann
313 Washington Street
Newton, MA 02158–1626
Tel: 617-928-2500
Fax: 617-928-2620

For information on all Digital Press publications available, contact our World Wide Web home page at: http://www.bh.com/digitalpress

Order number: EY–V429E–DP

10 9 8 7 6 5 4 3 2

Printed in the United States of America

Für Claudia

Contents

Illustrations

Figures

TABLES

Preface

I started working with electronic mail in 1985. My first exposure was twofold. On the one hand, I was assigned to a customer to help implement a project involving ALL-IN-1, Digital Equipment Corporation's best-selling electronic-mail system. And on the other hand, as a new employee to Digital, I soon learned how a company could rely extensively, and sometimes almost exclusively, on an electronic tool as a means for internal communication. Digital was ahead of its time. In recent years e-mail may have become a household word, but just a decade ago it was a foreign concept even for many computer specialists.

As it happened, my career became closely aligned with Digital's office automation products. When speculation surfaced that ALL-IN-1 3.2 would support MAILbus 400 and its SMTP (simplified mail transport protocol, although many people call it e-mail or Internet mail) gateway, I thought it was about time to learn about the two primary electronic mail backbone protocols, X.400 and SMTP. So I tried to get my hands on some introductory material on the subject. This was not as easy as I had imagined. Almost all the literature I found was esoteric and assumed knowledge of the standards and previous experience with mail backbones. It also relied on the wide realm of networking. This is definitely changing—you need only to take a look at the latest Microsoft Exchange documentation to find references to either protocol—but I still believe that there is a need to give some background to the subject of mail protocols.

The first of the mail backbone protocols is the X.400 suite, defined in 1984. It was then considered by most government agencies and telecommunications companies throughout the world to be the only viable standard.

While the Internet mail standards and Internet standards were initially lacking in comparison, the situation has changed dramatically in recent years. Many companies are switching from X.400 to the Internet standard, SMTP, and new backbones are implemented mostly with SMTP.

Audience

Let me start by giving an indication of who is not included in the intended audience of this book. This is easy because there is really only one group of people who I think will not benefit from a brief overview—experienced message handling system managers. They should already know everything covered here and much more.

But that leaves a lot of people. And as vain as I am, and as important as I think electronic mail is for the world, I will acknowledge that people who have nothing to do with mail backbones, and never expect to, will find my discussion very academic to say the least.

So I have narrowed down my primary audience to individuals with current or planned involvement in the management of X.400 and/or SMTP. Some who fall into this category include:

1. Electronic-mail managers currently working with a legacy mailing system and considering an extension to X.400 or SMTP. These legacy systems might include LAN-mail applications such as Microsoft Mail or cc:Mail, or host-based applications such as PROFS or ALL-IN-1/Message Router.
2. Managers of X.400 backbones considering a switch to SMTP and needing to fully understand the implications.
3. Administrators of Microsoft Exchange who need to better understand the standards behind their connectors.

4. Messaging managers in companies that currently have no X.400 or Internet connection and are considering or planning on implementing such a connection.
5. System or network managers who do not deal directly with the messaging system but need to understand it since they perform many activities peripheral to it.
6. Upper-level IT (information technology) managers who need to understand the concepts of their messaging system in order to better support their subordinates.
7. Software developers who need to enable their applications to work with X.400 or SMTP.

Structure

I am not expecting the readers of this book to have much background in electronic messaging and have tried to structure the content so that it moves progressively from a very superficial overview to a more in-depth treatment of some of the concepts. I hope that by the end you will feel comfortable with the product documentation and other references that I have included.

Before I cover the concepts behind mailing and directory protocols, I need to make sure that you have the necessary background for understanding them. This includes knowledge of mailing systems and functionality, as well as a grasp of how the underlying network operates. Many of you are undoubtedly already familiar with some of this material and may wish to skip or skim over the first two chapters. But for others, those chapters will provide an overview of the basics and bring them up to a level of understanding that I assume through the remainder of the book.

Particularly in the area of networking, I will keep my discussion short in order to remain within my defined scope. You may not feel like you have mastered the information, but it should be enough to get you through the book and follow other publications on the subject. Those who are still curious can consult the bibliography for some excellent texts on the subject.

Topic and Scope

There is a lot that could be said about SMTP, X.400 and X.500. If this book was to teach you everything there is to know about them, starting from ground zero and explaining everything in simple terms, it would need to be written by a team of authors and could fill thousands of pages. The result would be that very few people would have the stamina to read it from cover to cover.

I have chosen a less ambitious goal. I would like to acquaint the reader with the terminology and concepts of these standards. One problem I have with the protocols is that they are very abstract. They only become concrete when you have to deal with them repeatedly on a very practical and technical level in the real world. Needless to say, I can't give you that, but I have tried to provide some examples to help illustrate the concepts. In particular, I have chosen to reference Microsoft Exchange, MAILbus 400 and Digital X.500, since these are quite thorough and faithful implementations of the standards. It may well be that you will work with other products but, to the extent that they adhere to the standards, the functionality will be similar even if it is implemented differently.

References

Part of my objective is to provide you with a base for further developing your knowledge. I can't even begin to cover all the information there is on the subject and presenting any of it in too much detail would only distract from the overview. So, naturally, many of you will feel that I have exposed only the tip of the iceberg and that there is much more to be explored. Others may be content with an overview but not feel like they have fully understood one section or the other. If you are interested in a particular section, consult the references at the end of its chapter.

World Wide Web

One of the sources I found most informative while working on this book was the World Wide Web (WWW). To give you the benefit of my searches, I am including several references to WWW pages; however, some of these pages may no longer be available or may have moved by the time you read this book. If that happens, you can still try to search for the pages yourself using one of the Web search engines (e.g., http://www.altavista.digital.com/). You may even find more interesting Web pages than I have listed. Try entering SMTP or X.400 and follow all the links, and you will be busy for as long as you want.

Mail Address

During the course of writing this book I have worked out of Digital's offices in Austria, Ireland and Malaysa. I could have cleaned up my examples to all references to our e-mail system in Dublin, but I thought it would be more interesting to add some variety by using examples from wherever I happened to be. So don't be too confused if not all my e-mail addresses work. If you want to reach me, your best bet, at the time of publication, is: Rhoton@mail.dec.com.

Acknowledgments

I would like to express my appreciation to all those who have helped me, in various ways, to write this book. These include Werner Moser, who patiently explained many of the networking and mail protocols to me; Tony Redmond, who reviewed the manuscript and made a number of valuable suggestions for improvement; Liz McCarthy, who motivated me to continue writing to get the manuscript ready for production.

There are many others whom I must thank collectively, but of them all, I am most grateful to Claudia for her understanding while I spent much of the little free time I had working on this book.

Chapter 1
Introduction

Electronic Messaging: A Journey Through Time

Past

Some of the first systems for electronic communication (for example, the first versions of ALL-IN-1) were based on a single computer. Users would be able to send messages only to other accounts on the same machine. These messages would be stored in a repository, where they could be fetched by all of the specified recipients. This was a great achievement in its time. It meant that colleagues could send notices to each other from their desks. They no longer had to play telephone tag with each other to ensure that their associates received their urgent messages.

This is one of the defining characteristics of electronic messaging. Like the postal service, it provides an asynchronous transfer of data. Contrast this with a telephone conversation, which expects both participants to be connected at the same time.

Still, of course, there was a major limitation. While a single machine may well have accommodated a department, it was unlikely that a whole organization could have accounts together while providing acceptable response time. The mail system was restricted to local use, and when it was necessary to transmit information across the network, people resorted to copying files.

In response, the Internet took its first stab at the problem, extending the file transfer specifications to include structured mail messages. This solved the immediate problem but was far from ideal. File copies had no mechanism for notification and did not support many of the necessary mail features like distribution lists and structured attachments. Problems arose if one of the links on the path from the source to the destination was down. The user had to wait and retry later until the file could be accessed.

So the need developed to extend mail to the network. ALL-IN-1 version 2, for example, took advantage of Digital's Message Router product to provide a backbone for networked messaging. Message Router had a programmable interface that applications like ALL-IN-1 and MailWorks could call to deliver or collect mail. It took care of transferring the messages to the remote nodes by relaying them from one message router to another until they arrived at their destination.

Others solved the problem from a different angle. They wrote sophisticated programs to assist in file copying. They established a directory structure, often called a post office, that would help to categorize people's mail and often would also transfer additional files with information about the messages (such as who sent them, to whom and when they were sent, and their subject). With programs on each computer monitoring the directories, they could even program in support for notifications. This type of transfer is called a shared-file interface, since the same files are accessed by both the sending node (for writing) and the receiving node (for reading). MS Mail, cc:Mail and many other PC mail solutions use this type of interface because it is relatively easy to implement and provides a good level of functionality.

These approaches provided the functionality to link all of the users within an organization with each other regardless of their physical location or organizational position. However, the journey was not yet over. As each company developed its own mail applications, a number of software vendors had their own ideas about mail formats and protocols. With every company defining its own standards, there was bound to be chaos if a customer ever wanted to link together messaging systems from different vendors. Needless to say, there were such customers and there was chaos.

A new component, called a gateway, was introduced to solve the problem. This piece of software would help join together two heterogeneous mail systems by converting the format from one into that of the other, and vice versa. It could also speak the protocols of both of its peer systems, making it possible for them to communicate with each other.

The gateway helped fill the need for everyone in the world to communicate with each other. But there was one drawback. It was a lot of effort and rather complex. After all, it meant that you had to have a gateway for every type of mail system with which you wanted to communicate.

Of course, these were the same problems that had already been encountered with networks in general, which are also numerous and dissimilar. There you had DECnet, SNA, USENET, SDNET and BITNET, among others. To help solve the networking problem, a number of standards had been proposed that were intended to bring all of the networks together to follow a small set of protocols that could easily be supported by all.

This strategy was also adopted with regard to messaging. A committee from the group then called CCITT (Comité Consultatif International de Télégraphique et Téléphonique) and later renamed ITU–T (International Telecommunication Union–Telecommunications Standardization Sector) convened in 1984 and proposed what came to be known as the X.400 recommendations. They defined a set of protocols that could be used to implement homogeneous backbones that could interoperate regardless of who produced them. In principle, if everything had been defined and everyone adhered to the standards, this plan would work flawlessly. But even without that perfection, at least there was a common backbone that made it possible to interconnect messaging systems with minimal loss of functionality. This was already a great step forward.

In recognition of changing needs and technology, the ITU–T meets at regularly scheduled four-year intervals to defined new standards or revise old ones. In 1988 they revised the X.400 standard, making quite a few changes. I don't want to focus in on the differences here, since most systems today implement the 1988 version.[1] You should know, however, that the two protocols are not very compatible with each other. What this means is that the newer messaging backbones have to implement both protocols in order to be able to communicate with the older ones. A 1988 backbone is equipped with the knowledge of how to process a 1984 message, but not vice versa. So the 1988 backbone downgrade' its messages when sending them to a 1984 system. The 1984 standards were published in volumes with red covers, and the 1988 standards in ones with blue covers. In the trade they are therefore often referred to as the Red Book and the Blue Book, respectively.

Around the same time the IETF (Internet Engineering Task Force) also saw the need to define a protocol for mail backbones. In 1982 they produced two standards called RFC (request for comments) 821 and 822, respectively. These definitions are still in use today, and they dictate how mail is to be structured as well as transferred through the Internet. As we shall see, the standards have been supplemented by further refinement such as MIME (multipurpose Internet mail extensions) and security mechanisms.

Future

I will come back to the present shortly, but first let me venture a look into the future of messaging. My projections are speculative, of course. For all I know, tomorrow somebody will invent a revolutionary networking technology that will make everything we now know obsolete. On the other hand, it is possible that the current tendency will continue.

The Internet is growing at a staggering pace, and it looks as though at some point in the future it will supplant the OSI (open systems interconnect) networks. When it does, it is very likely that the Internet's mailing protocol, SMTP, will replace X.400.

The Web-enabling of mail applications has already opened the e-mail domain to the World Wide Web, as users are able to use a

---

[1] You can refer to Radicati (1992) for a clear discussion of the differences.

browser like Microsoft Internet Explorer or Netscape Navigator to access mail. It is no longer mandatory to have applications dedicated to e-mail and they may be in the process of disappearing. Some mail applications like Hotmail[2] are even tailored for Web access.

The question that remains open is how far this will go. Will e-mail servers and even backbones be supplanted in favor of Web services or other forthcoming technologies? Will mail backbones eventually become unnecessary in a world where bandwidth is increasingly becoming a commodity?

On another front, we may also see further development of EDI (electronic data interchange), which is closely related to electronic mail. EDI defines specific structures for financial documents such as purchase orders and invoices. These documents can be sent via electronic mail to other departments or, more importantly, other companies. Since the structure of the documents is agreed on, the recipients can make use of standard software to process the data being sent. EDI is currently burgeoning and, so far, it is more closely aligned with X.400 than with SMTP.

Another related emerging technology is groupware. In particular, workflow has the potential of strongly influencing electronic mail. Traditional electronic mail allows you to specify a list of recipients, all of whom receive your message shortly after you send it. Usually this is what you want. But workflow would give you added abilities to route your message to a set of recipients in sequence. Each one might be able to modify an attached document or perform other related transactions. Then the message or workflow item would be passed on to the next recipient.

Present

So where does that leave us for the present? Is it worth investing in X.400 with the Internet standard just around the corner? Well, in the end, every company will need to decide that on a case-by-case basis. It

[2] Hotmail is free Web-based e-mail available at http://www.hotmail.com.

is hardly imaginable that a company looking into electronic mail at this time would not want an Internet connection. But there are some good reasons for considering the support of X.400 in addition to Internet:

1. You may need to communicate with someone who has access to only one of the services. With both backbones in place, you give your users the ability to send mail into both worlds. In some cases (when addressing to people who have both) you benefit only in the event of a failure along the primary path. In other cases, however, your users may need to communicate with people who really have only one type of mail system.
2. You may want the additional functionality and layered applications associated with one system. If you want to implement EDI, for instance, you will find it much easier to use X.400, since the EDI standard (X.435) is based on an X.400 network.
3. You may want to hedge your bets for the future. While it may look now like the Internet is poised to oust the OSI protocols, we all know how dynamic and unpredictable the computer market really is. It would only take a new technology that is better suited to the X.400 approach than to the Internet, and everything could be up for grabs again.
4. The present may last a long time. Technology has a tendency to change at a breathtaking pace, but businesses have a habit of not keeping up. You can be sure that a lot of companies that have a working X.400 backbone will be reluctant to throw it out on a whim to replace it with the latest item on the technology fashion list. There are still businesses that run with telex machines and typewriters. If the glitter of the newest technology could not dislodge those, it will have a tough time with investment-intensive systems like X.400.

International Standards

Standardization is not exactly the most exciting topic with which to start a book. The standards themselves have never made any bestseller lists either. I wouldn't blame you if you wanted to skip this chapter and go on to the next. And yet X.400 and SMTP are themselves sets of standards, and any discussion of them inevitably touches on a few others. If standards were few and simple, a couple of paragraphs might suffice to orient the reader. But, alas, they are neither, and so I am afraid I will have to indulge in a short excursion into this weird and wonderful world.

First and foremost, you should always keep in mind that standards are developed by some of the most renowned experts in the field after careful study and extensive discussion. If at times they seem odd, inconsistent, or unnecessary, it is because you don't understand them and need to study them in more detail.

That is what I used to think, anyhow. Then I took at look at some of them and read a few commentaries. I won't admit that I changed my mind, but if you read between the lines you may notice some occasional skepticism on my part regarding the standardization process. To avoid any misunderstanding, I should clarify that I do feel the people and organizations developing the standards are doing a great job. I just don't believe perfection is possible when it comes to getting millions of people to agree and do the same thing.

Standards are still necessary, of course. Without them no two pieces of software or equipment would ever work together if different people had developed them. We would even have difficulty describing the functionality of complete products without commonly accepted terms and definitions. So a certain amount of homogeneity is indispensable in an efficient world.

And yet there are some fundamental problems with any attempts to define norms. We must agree on who should do the norming. The norms must always reflect the current state of their domain and they should not be unnecessarily complex.

Interdependencies

It is all very well to say that norms should not be complex, but in reality they must often define numerous multifaceted interactions. This poses a dilemma. The most elegant solution to such a problem is to break down the complexity. There are often existing standards that can be applied to some portions of the domain, and it is easier to integrate these standards than to duplicate them.

This sounds very nice and is incontestably the best way to go, but it does create its own problems. It makes implementation more difficult when there is no single source to a standard but rather a maze of interconnections. It also makes the standard more vulnerable to changes when some of the underlying references are modified. Our standards are like a house of playing cards. You have to be very careful if you decide to move one of them at the base, or the whole house will collapse. In mail, as we will see, if we throw out the OSI model not much of X.400 will be left standing. Similarly, changing IP (Internet protocol) could impact TCP (transmission control protocol), thereby affecting SMTP and even MIME.[3]

Changing Technology

Information technology changes very rapidly. This presents an obvious problem to standardization. It is difficult, if not impossible, to foresee what functional developments may take place that would need to be considered when specifying certain interfaces and protocols. The utilization of technology can be very dynamic as new uses are considered for existing functionality.

We can respond to these changes proactively or reactively. A proactive approach attempts to foresee areas of potential changes and accommodates these by leaving certain points open. We can say that the specification then becomes abstract because it does not dictate a concrete instance but permits an open-ended choice of implementations. This approach offers the advantage that the standard can be extended without being modified, but the lack of specification makes understanding the standard a great deal more difficult. And this latter point is one of

3 With careful planning it is, of course, possible to reduce or eliminate the impact on other protocols, as has been done with IPv6. This is not an easy task, however.

the charges that is often made against many of the ISO (International Organization for Standardization) and ITU standards. They are too abstract to understand and implement consistently.

A reactive approach means that the standards need to be periodically revised in order to be applicable. It also can mean that certain norms will become outdated, as their bases become obsolete, and that new standards will appear in their place. So learning a standard is never a completed act. You might know and implement it at a given point in time, but you are always aware of the fact that it is going to either change or be superseded by another standard that does.

Another issue is that it takes time to recognize the need for a standard, to define a response to the need, to achieve a consensus on the response, to publish it as a standard and to implement the standard. One disadvantage of this is that it takes a while to get the functionality in a standard form, and by then you may not even need it, or you may need something different. Possibly a more serious problem is that not everyone will wait on the standard. Some developers may decide it is worth using the interval to develop a nonstandard solution that customers can use in the interim. If they are successful, they may capture the market and establish their approach as the de facto standard. By the time the de jure standard is available, nobody may want it.

Standards Bodies

Imagine a world with a global, centrally administered organization in charge of establishing norms for everything we produce and consume. Nobody challenges the standards they create, and everyone adheres to them without reservation. It sounds a great deal like the place envisaged in a certain George Orwell book. I am not sure if he knew that the X.400 standards would be defined in the year that he describes.

In any case, at present we are in no danger of this happening. Whenever there is something to norm, one group will come up with a specification that, for various reasons, someone else will challenge with alternatives. I do not wish to imply that the relationship between the normative agencies is adversarial (they often cooperate quite closely and some times coauthor joint standards). They do, however, attempt to influence the norms from a particular perspective, and emphasize certain areas over others. For the expert familiar with the history of organizations and their standardizing processes, there are few surprises. But a first glance at the specifications in their entire number and volume can certainly be intimidating.

I wish to say only a few short words about some of the primary agencies so that you know who I am talking about when I reference them later.[4]

ITU

The ITU (International Telecommunication Union) is an "international organization within which governments and the private sector coordinate global telecom networks and services" (http://www.itu.ch/). It is divided into sectors, of which the most important for us is the ITU–T (International Telecommunication Union–Telecommunications Standardization Sector), formerly called CCITT (Comité Consultatif International de Télégraphique et Téléphonique). Be aware that a lot of older and even some newer documentation still refer to the standards, as CCITT standards so this name is not just a piece of trivia.

The ITU–T publishes recommendations that are categorized into series. There is one series for each letter of the alphabet and it represents a specific technological domain. Messaging falls under the Series X recommendations, "Data networks and open system communications." This is where the X.400 standards on message handling systems (X.400-X.485) and the X.500 standards on directory services (X.500-X.582) are defined, as well as a number of standards relating to networking, X.25 being probably the best-known.

[4] You can find a larger, albeit still far from exhaustive, list of organizations in Martin and Leben (1992: 27), and many remarks on some of the bodies in Tanenbaum (1996).

Just to keep you on your toes, the ITU has doubly assigned the X.400 standard. In case you become disoriented and start looking under Series F recommendations, "Non-telephone Telecommunications Services," you will find one called F.400.

ISO

ISO (International Organization for Standardization) is a "worldwide federation of national standards bodies" (http://www.iso.ch/infoe/intro.html). You may be tempted to correlate the three initials of the full name with the short form ISO. There is a strange similarity there, and one could easily imagine that in Latin or Esperanto the same words are ordered differently. However, if you go to the library to look it up, I suggest you start with a Greek dictionary, where you will find that *isos* means "equal." The name is meant to imply that standards make all implementations equal—at least in some respects.

ISO has developed a multitude of standards in almost every field imaginable. The photographers among you have probably seen ISO's ratings for film speeds, Europeans know what the paper size A4 means, and most of the world is familiar with the metric symbols like *kg* or *m*. Of particular interest to us is the OSI (Open Systems Interconnect) model of networking, which we will encounter later on.

If you compare the ISO and ITU–T recommendations in the areas of networking, you will find a fair amount of overlap. It might have been easier if they would have simply cross-referenced each other rather than giving each norm a new name, but that is not what happened. In any case, generally only one of the names is used in the industry, so there is little confusion in practice.

For X.400 the ISO standard is almost identical to the ITU–T's 1988 version. This is an example of two bodies working together to produce a joint specification. There are some minor differences, such as the documentation of private extensions by ISO, but you will rarely find anyone distinguishing between them, and everyone calls the protocol by its ITU–T name, X.400.

X/OPEN

X/Open calls itself a "not-for-profit, vendor-independent, international consortium, which is dedicated to the advancement of open systems throughout the world" (http://www.xopen.org/5minute.htm). It issues specifications that are adopted into its common application environment (CAE). Of interest to us are:

- C609 API to Electronic Mail (X.400), Issue 3
- C608 API to Directory Services (XDS), Issue 3
- C305 Message Store API
- C607 OSI-Abstract-Data Manipulation API (XOM), Issue 3

C609 is usually known as XAPI (X.400 Application Programming Interface) and it, as well as the others, is a joint specification with XAPIA (X.400 Application Programmers Interface Association).

As you might guess from the name, XAPI will allow you to write programs (user agents) that communicate with X.400 components. XDS (X/Open API to Directory Services) gives you an interface for programs (directory user agents) to connect to X.500 components. For both of these, you need to work with abstract OSI-defined objects (such as messages or directory entries) that can be represented using a very complex structure, as we shall see later on. To make it a bit easier, XOM (X/Open API for OSI-Abstract-Data Manipulation) can assist in creating and manipulating these objects.

The X/Open specifications will probably be of interest to you only if you are doing programming. Each of these specifications, as well as a guide (G150) introducing the X.400 and directory services APIs, may be ordered from X/Open. If you look up the Web page indicated above, you will find links to the list of standards, as well as the ISBNs with which to order them.

OIW

OIW (Open Systems Environment Implementers Workshop) (http://www.oiw.org/) helps define agreements on the implementation of some of the OSI standards. When a consensus has been reached, the agreements are termed "stable" and are known in the industry as the Stable Implementers Agreements.

IETF

The IETF (Internet Engineering Task Force) is the "protocol engineering and development arm of the Internet" (http://www.ietf.cnri.reson.va.us/home). It is open to participation by anyone who is interested in contributing to evolution of Internet architecture. Among other things, it produces official documents that are sequentially numbered and called RFCs (request for comments).[5]

There are various types of RFCs referred to as informational, experimental, historic and standards track. We are primarily interested in the latter, which define the official protocols, although the others often provide very useful background information. Within the standards track, RFCs may be classified according to the stage in the standardization process as proposed standard, draft standard or Internet standard.[6]

Table 1-1 lists some of the RFCs that we will discuss. Once published as Internet standards, the RFCs do not change. Instead, if they are found to be inadequate or if corrections need to be made, other RFCs (with new numbers) are submitted to take their place. Looking at the previous RFCs can often give you an idea of the evolution of the standard through time. In some cases it may be helpful to start by looking at the original RFC, which is often simpler, and then progress to the current version of the standard.

---

[5] The RFCs are available on the Internet at ftp://ds.internic.net/rfc/ and are mirrored to a number of sites around the Internet.

[6] If you look at RFC 2000, which contains the standardization state of the various RFCs, you will find a dual categorization of the RFCs. The state of an RFC refers to its "maturity level," (e.g., "standard," "draft standard," "proposed standard," "experimental," "informational" or "historic.") The status is the "requirement level" of the protocol, (e.g., "required," "recommended," "elective," "limited use," or "not recommended.") You will find much more information on the Internet standardization process in RFCs 1786, 1800, 1818 and 2000.

Table 1-1. *Requests for Comments (RFCs)*

Area	RFC	Previous RFCs	Description
Network	768		User Datagram Protocol (UDP)
	791	760	Internet Protocol (IP aka IPv4)
	793	761, 675	Transmission Control Protocol (TCP)
	882		Domain Names — Concepts and Facilities
	883		Domain Names — Implementation and Specification
	974		Mail Routing and the Domain System
	1006	983	ISO Transport Service on Top of the TCP
	1700	1340, 1060, 1010, 990, 960, 943, 923, 900, 870, 820, 790, 776, 770, 762, 758, 755, 750, 739, 604, 503, 433, 349	Assigned Numbers
	1883		Internet Protocol , Version 6 (IPv6)
General	959	765	File Transfer Protocol (FTP)
	977		Network News Transfer Protocol (NNTP)
	2068	1945	Hypertext Transfer Protocol (HTTP)
Mail	821	788, 780, 772	Simple Mail Transfer Protocol (SMTP)
	822	733, 724, 680, 561	Format of ARPA Internet Text Messages
	1327	1148, 1138, 1026, 987	Mapping Between X.400(1988) / ISO 10021 and RFC 822
	1494		Equivalencies Between (1988) X.400 and RFC 822 Message Bodies
	1495		Mapping Between X.400 and RFC 822 Message Bodies
	1502		X.400 Use of Extended Character Sets
	1939	1725, 1460, 1225, 1081, 937-POP2, 918-POP	Post Office Protocol — Version 3
	2045–2049	1522, 1521,1341, 934	(Message Encapsulation), 1049 (Content-types) Multipurpose Internet Mail Extensions
	2060	1730	Internet Message Access Protocol — Version 4rev1 (IMAP4)
Directory	1777	1487	Lightweight Directory Access Protocol
Security	1421–1424	1114, 1115, 1040, 989	Privacy Enhancement for Internet Electronic Mail
	1847		Security Multiparts for MIME
	1848		MIME Object Security Services
	2015		MIME Security with Pretty Good Privacy (PGP)

Unlike the OSI and ITU standards, the RFCs are available for public access on the World Wide Web at numerous locations.

Primary Standards for Electronic Messaging

Table 1-2. *Summary of Standards*

Organization	Standard	Description
ITU–T	F.400	Messaging Handling Systems
	T.51	Latin-Based Coded Character Sets for Telematic Services
	T.61	Teletex Character Set
	T.101	International Interworking for Videotex Services
	X.400	Messaging Handling Systems
	X.500	Directory Services
	X.25	Packet Switching Interface
	X.121	X.25 DTE Addresses
ISO	6937	Coded Graphic Character Set for Text Communication — Latin Alphabet
	8824	Abstract Syntax Notation One (ASN.1)
	8825	Basic Encoding Rules
	8859	ISO Latin Character Set
	10021	GeneralText Character Set
	10646	Universal Multiple-Octet Coded Character Set (UCS)
X/Open	C609	API to Electronic Mail (X.400)
	C608	API to Directory Services (XDS)
	C305	Message Store API
	C607	OSI Abstract Data Manipulation API (XOM)
IETF	RFC 791	Internet Protocol (IP)
	RFC 793	Transmission Control Protocol (TCP)
	RFC 821	Simple Mail Transport Protocol (SMTP)
	RFC 822	Format of Electronic Mail Messages
	RFC 1006	ISO Transport Services on Top of TCP
	RFC 1327	Mapping Between X.400 and RFC 822
	RFC 1494	Equivalencies Between 1988 X.400 and RFC 822 Message Bodies
	RFC 1495	Mapping Between X.400 and RFC 822
	RFC 1777	Lightweight Directory Access Protocol (LDAP)
	RFC 1939	Post Office Protocol — Version 3 (POP3)
	RFC 2045–2049	Multipurpose Internet Mail Extensions (MIME)
	RFC 2060	Internet Message Access Protocol — Version 4rev1 (IMAP4)

Functionality for the User

Most people have an idea of the typical functionality that an e-mail system offers. You can compose a message and send if off to a friend or colleague, who may read it the next day and send a reply back. That is the basic function of a mailing system, and pretty much all applications offer this and much more. I would like to take a quick look at what an X.400 conform mail application offers to the end-user so that we can have a better idea of what the implementation is trying to accomplish.

Structured Bodyparts

An X.400 message can contain multiple bodyparts, allowing you to structure and compartmentalize your message in some logical form. You can isolate different types of data from each other and manipulate them separately. These bodyparts are also referred to as the message text and its attachments. In most cases the attachments can be serially attached to the message, and the recipient will simply extract or view the bodyparts of interest.

But in some cases you may wish for a more complex structure. I am sure you can think of examples in your use of mail, but just to illustrate my point, imagine that you have sales data from various geographical areas. It is available in raw form from the individual locations and summarized by region. Figure 1-1 illustrates how this structure might look. You could just string the sections together and the recipient would still have the same data, but it would be nice to maintain the structure. X.400 does this by allowing the structure of the bodyparts to be defined hierarchically.

SMTP does not know anything about bodyparts. Its smallest unit is a seven-bit ASCII message that it transfers from one user to another. This is clearly a disadvantage compared to X.400's capabilities and was actually a reason for (particularly European) interest in X.400. In the past few years, with binary fields from various PC applications flying around the network, such a restriction could have meant the death of SMTP.

But here is an illustration of the responsive nature of the Internet. When the need was felt for a complex eight-bit bodypart structure, MIME was developed. It is currently defined in RFCs 2045 through 2049. It provides a mechanism to pack multiple 8-bit

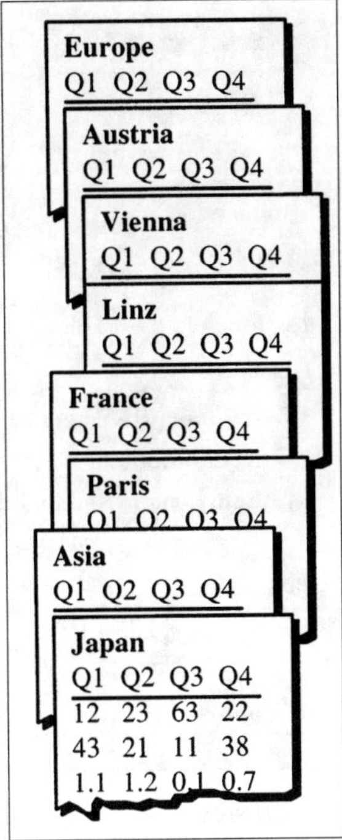

Figure 1-1. *Hierarchical Bodyparts*

attachments into seven-bit messages and thus allowed SMTP to get back into the game.

Message Attributes

All mail systems associate attributes with the messages. At the very least, you need to know the recipients of the message, and you almost always have the ability to specify a subject. There are, however, many more items that can be defined. Figure 1-2 shows some of the X.400 characteristics that can be specified when creating a message. Most of these characteristics and several others are defined by X.400 and SMTP, and you will find them in any compliant mail application; however, X.400 defines a few more than SMTP (RFC 822).

Following are descriptions of many of the basic attributes that may be defined by most X.400 mail systems:

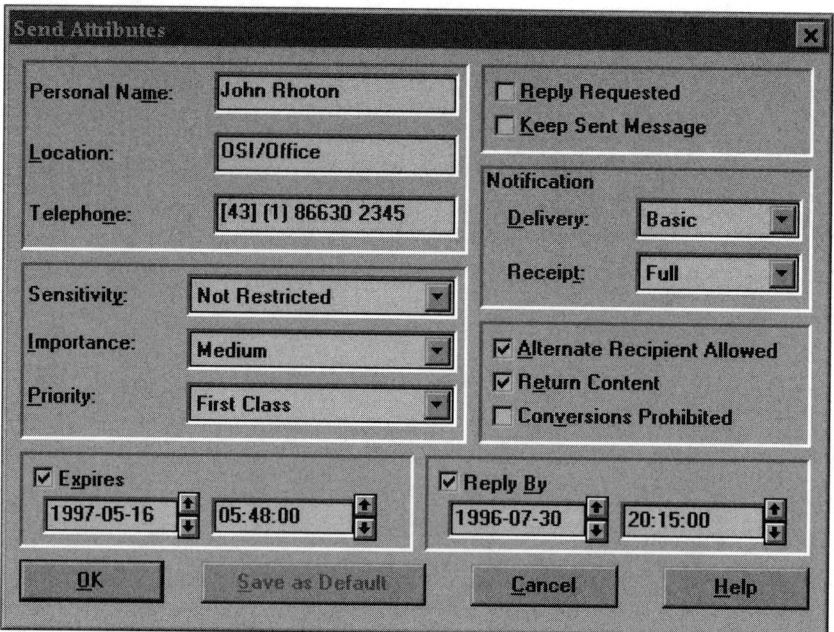

Figure 1-2. *X.400 Message Attributes in TeamLinks*

- **Personal name:** This is purely informational, to help your correspondent identify you.
- **Location:** This is also informational for the recipient.
- **Telephone:** Again, this is informational for the recipient.
- **Sensitivity:** This attribute is only informational as far as X.400 is concerned. However, there is nothing to stop a given piece of mail software for using the field to implement restrictions in what the user is allowed to do with messages. For example, it might make sense not to allow someone to forward company confidential or personal mail outside the corporation. The four sensitivity fields are:
  - Not restricted
  - Personal
  - Private
  - Company Confidential

- **Importance:** This again is only informational for X.400. The mail application may elect to use the field to require users to read urgent mail, or it may be less dictatorial and simply flag urgent messages so that the user can attend to them first. Alternatively, some systems might implement a mail filter with which the user can have all low-priority messages refiled without reading or have urgent messages forwarded to another location during absence. The possible values for importance are:
  - Low
  - Medium
  - Urgent
- **Priority:** Finally we have one that is not necessarily only informational as far as the mail delivery subsystem is concerned. The idea is that, similarly to traditional mail, you should have the option of paying more to have your letter arrive sooner, or saving money when time is not an issue. How this is implemented is determined by the messaging backbone. It could just ignore the priority, particularly if there is no charge per message. On the other hand, it might favor the higher-priority messages during times of congestion or connect to other mail systems at shorter intervals when express messages are waiting. We have three priority classes:
  - Express
  - First Class
  - Second Class
- **Expiry Date:** You might have a message that you don't want the recipient to see unless it is read before a certain date. For example, you might suggest going out for dinner this evening to an old friend. But if she doesn't read it by this evening, then it won't do her or you much good. And she might even mistake it for a dinner invitation tomorrow if that is when she reads it. To prevent this, you could set an expiry date for today at 19:00 and hope she sees it before then.

- **Reply requested:** You could specify that your correspondent should reply to your message. Again, the implementation at the other end could be very strict and require, the recipient to enter a response, even if it is only meaningless gibberish. Or it could be lax and merely inform the user that a reply is requested.
- **Delivery notification:** You can use this field if you want to know whether or not your messages are being delivered. There are three possible values:
    - Basic notification, which informs you whenever a message cannot be delivered to its intended recipient.
    - Full notification, which informs you of success or failure with an appropriate report. This can be useful if you want to make absolutely sure your message arrives; for example, so that you can try alternative means of contact if you have the wrong address or the connection is not operational.

      Once you have received the success notification you know you can relax. Until then you cannot be positive that your message has arrived.
    - No notification (none), which you might use if you are sending messages to a number of people who are all only intermittently available. You would like them to receive the message but aren't too concerned if the odd address is not working. And you definitely don't want to be bothered by it.
- **Receipt notification:** This is fairly similar to delivery notification but operates on receipt (when the user reads or manipulates the message) rather than on delivery (when the message is delivered to user's account). Again you have three possible values:
    - Basic notification will send you a report if the message cannot be received (e.g., the account is closed).
    - If full is specified, you will always receive a report when the user processes the message.
    - None means you do not want to be notified of receipt.
- **Alternate recipient allowed:** If this is specified, your message might be automatically forwarded to an alternate address if it cannot be sent to the intended recipient.

- **Return content:** Some times delivery of a message will fail and you will receive a notification. You can specify here whether the notification should include your original message (e.g., so that you can resend it to another address).
- **Conversions prohibited:** Many message transport systems utilize a set of converters to ensure that bodyparts are sent to the recipients in formats they can understand. This makes it easier on the recipients when they don't have to perform the conversion themselves or be faced with formats they cannot use. But in some cases, you may not trust the converters, or you may have reason to send a message to someone in a format he does not ordinarily receive. By specifying this attribute, you can be sure the message will not be converted. Either it will pass to the user in its original form, or you will be notified that it cannot be delivered as specified.
- **Reply-by date:** This option gives you the opportunity to indicate to your recipient that you expect a reply by a certain time. The application may notify the user of this request or even make an attempt to insist that the user reply. Obviously, it is ultimately up to your correspondent to honor the request.
- **Deferral date:** This attribute allows you to defer the delivery of a message to a specified time in the future. You might want to use this to remind someone (including yourself) of some event. Or you might simply want to make sure you send the message, but also want to reserve the option of modifying it until the last moment. You can cancel a deferred message until the time it is delivered. If you don't, or if you wait too long, it will go on to the recipient like any other message.

Those are some of the properties you can assign to your X.400 message. The set of properties of SMTP messages is much more loosely defined. We shall see some of them in Chapter 3. As you will have noticed, a great deal depends on the implementation of the mail software that you are using. To find out exactly what you can specify and what impact it will have in your mail environment, you will need to refer to the documentation associated with your application.

Message Correlation

X.400 interpersonal messages are associated with a globally unique identification called the IPMID (interpersonal message identification). By referencing this I.D. it is possible to correlate messages with each other. For example, we can say that message Y is a reply to my message X. If my user agent has the facility, I can have it look for my message X to find out what my correspondent is talking about.

The IPMD can also be useful for notification correlation. If I send out a message and want to know whether and when all the users have received it, I can indicate that I wish to have delivery notifications. But trying to make sense of hundreds of notifications could be a tiresome job. Fortunately, since the notifications specify the IPMID to which they refer, the whole process can be automated by the user agent.

Addressing

One of the primary properties of a message is its list of recipients. Both SMTP and X.400 allow you to specify three kinds of recipients, called "To," "CC" and "BCC."

There is no technical difference between To and CC (carbon copy), other than recipients appearing in one list or the other. The difference is rather somewhat historical. Back in the ancient time of typewriters, it was customary to type letters to several people at once with the pages separated by carbon sheets. One person would be considered the primary addressee and would receive the original, while the others would get the carbon copies. In the age of electronics we no longer have such technical limitations, but it can still be useful to distinguish between primary and secondary recipients of our messages. The term *courtesy copy* is sometimes used nowadays to reflect the change in meaning.

BCC (blind carbon copy) carries the same implication as CC but entails an important technical difference. BCC recipients receive the message just like anyone else, but they do not appear in the addressee list. You would use this when you want someone to receive the message but don't want anyone else to know that this person has received the message. This option might sound a bit misleading, and you may not see any legitimate use for it.

Even before the days of BCC, the same thing was accomplished in a different way. All you needed to do was take the message you had already sent and forward it to some one else. The original recipients would be none the wiser, and your secret correspondent could read the message. BCC just makes the process easier and elegant, since you don't have multiple messages to track.

Directory Services

Very closely tied to X.400, which defines mailing, is another standard called X.500, which specifies directory services.

I have mentioned the various types of recipients so far without indicating how they are specified. In any mailing system, you enter the addressee by typing in his address. What differs between mail types is the syntax of the address. In an X.400 system you would enter a recipient in a format similar to:

```
C=AT; A=ADA; P=Digital; O=Digital; OU=AUI; CN=John Rhoton;
```

This syntax may or may not seem cryptic to you. We will look at the format in more detail a little later, but what is important now is that it is unlikely that you will remember a fifty character address for every person you want to send a message to. After all, you probably don't remember many people's postal addresses either, but instead look them up in an address book when you need to send a letter. Even if you can remember the address, software is notorious for demanding precision. All it would take would be to type in a comma somewhere instead of a semicolon, and your message would never make it to its destination. Most conventional post offices are more forgiving in this respect.

This is where it can be very useful to have a directory service. In its simplest form it is just an electronic version of your address book and is actually called a personal address book (PAB). But that does not exploit the full potential of electronic directories. In a PAB you need to enter all the information yourself. This is not really a problem if you have a small, static list of people to whom you regularly send messages. But you will probably want to correspond with a constantly changing set of people. And if you don't know their address, it's a little difficult to get started. After all, you can't send them messages asking them for their addresses.

Directory servers attempt to provide a nearly exhaustive list of possible addressees. Everyone you could possibly want to send a letter to should be there. Of course, this is an ambitious goal and one which will not soon be attained, but it is possible for an organization to enter all of its employees as well as some of their primary external contacts.

So now you have a database with entries for many of the people to whom you might want to send messages. You give the server the name of the person you want to reach and it will return the address to your mail application, which will insert it into your list of Tos, CCs or BCCs. That sure is a lot easier than filling in the syntax above. Or is it?

If you have a small list of entries then it almost certainly is, since you will not have many people with the same name, and typing in the name is easier than typing in the address. But imagine that your database contains all the employees in your company and is linked to other databases in other companies, so that, directly and indirectly, you have tens or hundreds of thousands of entries. The idea behind X.500 is that ultimately all the X.500 directories in the world could be linked together, and you could look up anyone who has an electronic mail account. It won't happen today or tomorrow, but it is likely that someday, some directory service will be globally defined and integrated.

What does this imply for us? First of all, it means that we need to think about what kind of key we are using for the database. If we just use the name, it won't know which John Smith we mean when we say we want to send something to John Smith. We need to find a way to uniquely identify our John Smith by indicating where he works and lives, but if we don't watch out we will have just as much trouble specifying how to look up John in the database as we would have entering his address manually!

But don't despair. What I have described so far is not really a directory server, but a name server. You give it a name and it looks up the name and returns a value, namely the address. Name servers are often used to look up node addresses from node names. But for people, we usually prefer to use directory servers. A directory server has more than just a name key and a value. It also lets you specify additional fields for each entry. So we might have something like you see in Table 1-3:

Table 1-3. *Directory Entry*

Field	Value
Common Name	John
Surname	Rhoton
Country	Malaysia
City	Kuala Lumpur
Address	4 Jalan Bersatu 13/4
Phone	60 3 751 3269
Company	Wisma Digital

Now all you need to do is enter values in enough of the fields to make the entry unique. In fact, you don't really need to do that. If the directory finds more than one matching entry, it returns them all and lets you either narrow your search with more search criteria or pick an item from the list.

Note that it is up to your applications and organization to decide what data to enter on each person. While the above would be some of the typical fields, you may instead want to enter completely different data on people. Maybe you want to be able to search for all American men born in Turkey in 1963. The possibilities depend on what you put in the database and what your directory applications will let you search for.

Usually when we think of X.500 directories, we think of the personal data that is stored in them. But they can store much more than that. In the case of MAILbus 400, a large amount of the configuration data is stored in X.500. You can also create entries for resources like printers and services. Once you have the X.500 infrastructure in place, it is just a question of adding information to the database and providing a means to access it.

One other important point about an X.500 directory is that it is hierarchical. So far I have discussed it as though it were a linear set of entries, and for all intents and purposes, a user can think of it as that. The implementation is a hierarchical tree, however. All entries, except the root, have a superior reference, and many have a subordinate reference. But we will look at that in more detail later.

The Internet has not defined a standard for directory services. Instead it offers a simplified interface to X.500 called LDAP (lightweight directory access protocol). We will be looking at this mechanism later in this book.

Highlights

- Three organizations have been the primary designers of today's e-mail backbones.
- ITU–T and ISO have defined a structured, formal architecture.
- IETF has designed a simple, implementation-oriented technology.
- The resulting backbones, X.400 and SMTP, are the two most prevalent in the world.
- Both offer similar functionality.
- They have vastly different approaches.
- They are not compatible with each other.
- The future looks brighter for SMTP.

References

To learn more about the standards bodies you can consult their home pages:

ITU	http://www.itu.ch/
ISO	http://www.iso.ch/
X/Open	http://xoweb.xopen.org
OIW	http://www.oiw.org/
IETF	http://www.ietf.cnri.reston.va.us

For an interesting perspective on the standards, see section 1.7 in:

Tanenbaum, Andrew S. 1996. *Computer Networks.* Englewood Cliffs, N.J.: Prentice Hall. ISBN 0-13-394248-1.

For a list of standards organizations, see pages 26–35 in:

Martin, James, and Joe Leben. 1992. *DECnet Phase V: An OSI Implementation.* Boston: Digital Press. ISBN 1-5558-076-9.

One book to help you with the X.400 standard is:

Radicati, S. 1992. *Electronic Mail: An Introduction to the X.400 Message Handling Standards.* New York: McGraw-Hill. ISBN 0-07-051104-7.

For information on the Internet standardization process, see:

Huitema, C. 1995. *Not All RFCs Are Standards* (RFC 1796).

Postel, J. 1995. *Best Current Practices* (RFC 1818).

Postel, J. 1995. *Internet Official Protocol Standards* (RFC 1800).

Chapter 2

Networking

It would be possible to write quite a number of books on networks. In fact, some people already have. So rather than reinvent the wheel, I will summarize some of the points of particular significance to X.400 and SMTP.

Standards are useful in industry for almost every product, but nowhere are they more vital than when they describe an interface between components from different producers. This is the very essence of networking, or the connection of computing equipment.

While stand-alone computers may have been popular and sufficient some time ago, those days are gone. Outside of exceptionally stringent security needs, it is unthinkable for anyone to have a computer that cannot be connected to any others.

It might be nice if all of the vendors would just get together and design a standard piece of networking software that could be installed on every computer, allowing it to communicate with any other. We all know that won't happen, though. And the problem is not a conspiracy to keep people confused.

One problem is the issue of the different needs of different applications. Some may need highly reliable data delivery, while others are satisfied with a valiant attempt. Some may need a strict ordering of data, while others just want it to arrive there. In some cases, segments of data should arrive together or not at all.

Besides differing needs, we also have different means with which to work. To exploit their full potential, we need to use different procedures. There is a wide variety of physical media available with varying characteristics such as transmission time, bandwidth, and error rate.

OSI Layers

So on the one hand, it isn't possible to have just one networking mechanism. But on the other hand, we can't let every application define its own way of communicating with its peers. After all, we usually have only one network channel, and it would be very confusing if every program did with it as it saw fit. All the other connected nodes, and even the other applications on the same node, would constantly be bumping into each other.

The solution to this problem is found in a layered model. A layer is a software module; that is about all we know about it in terms of its implementation. A layer may share a process with other layers, or it may span several processes. It may be activated on demand or permanently loaded. We don't care too much about all that. What we want is to segment the network functionality so that we can easily replace one component with another that offers the same functions but uses a different implementation.

Layered networking models have been around for a while, but they used to divide the functionality in the layers differently from one model to another. This did not make the job of interoperability any easier, so ISO developed a standard model, which you see pictured in Figure 2-1. It is called the OSI (open systems interconnect) model and is now used almost universally for describing any kind of network implementation.

The selection of layers in a networking model is not an easy task. There are many different types of networks, and it is quite possible to implement them with very different architectures. Each layer needs to encompass a significant amount of functionality in order to describe

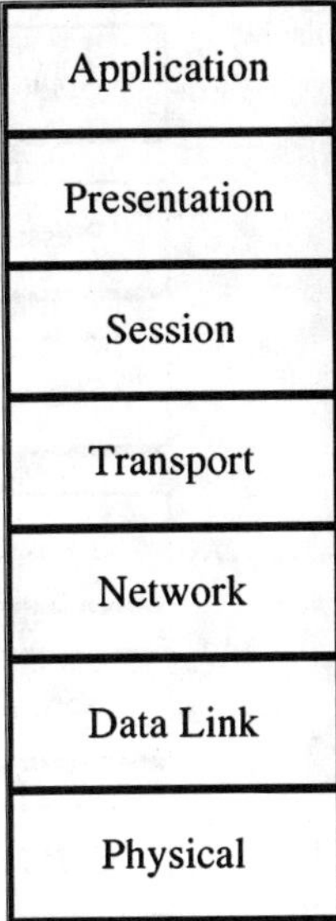

Figure 2-1. *OSI Layers*

a robust network. This means that either we need a lot of layers or each layer has to do a lot.

The architects of the OSI model strove for a simple structure. They decided on a set of criteria with which to make the essentially arbitrary choice of how to decide on the layers:

1. A layer involves one (necessary level of abstraction).
2. Interaction between adjacent layers is kept to a minimum.
3. Layers encompass internationally defined and accepted protocols.
4. A layer performs a well-defined function.

The objective was to limit the number of layers and only to introduce those that met the above criteria.

Of course, these models are not called *layers* for no reason. As you can see illustrated in Figure 2-2, the application, which is represented as the highest layer in the model and is the only part not provided by the network, calls the layer below it, in this case the presentation layer. Each layer passes the call on until we get to the physical layer, which

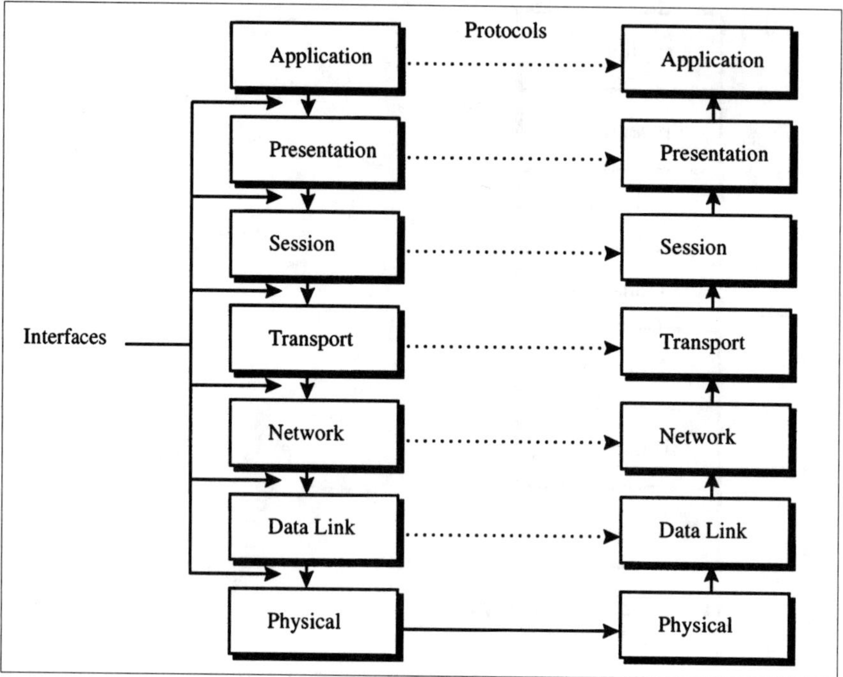

Figure 2-2. *OSI Protocols and Interfaces*

passes the data across the physical medium to the physical layer on the other system. There the data is passed up through the layers until it is given to the application on the other side.

We refer to the calls each of the layers makes to the adjacent layer as interfaces, which occur at service access points (SAPs). There is a SAP for each of the layers except the highest. So you may occasionally see references made to the NSAP (network service access point) or TSAP (transport service access point).

In Figure 2-2, you can also see dotted lines from each layer to its peer on the other system. The data that is passed (indirectly through the lower layers) conforms to a certain protocol. This means that in a given transmission, the data that is passed from the application layer to the presentation layer on the source system is the same data that is passed from the presentation layer to the application layer on the target system. The data in one transmission is called a protocol data unit (PDU) and again we have PDUs at each layer (e.g., APDUs, PPDUs, and SPDUs).

From the diagram, you can imagine the data following the arrows from one application layer all the way to the other. So it should be the same data. It is not quite that simple, though. The data passed from the application to the session layer is not the same as that passed from the session layer to the transport layer. Otherwise we wouldn't need all the intermediate layers—we could call the physical layer directly from the application.

Each layer manipulates the data in some way. It may add some information as a checksum, for instance. It could encrypt or compress the data. It could even do more complex things like dividing up the data and passing it on in multiple calls, or it could collect several units of data and combine them into one.

Our application doesn't really care what the various layers do to its data on the way. The important thing is that on the way back, each layer has to reverse the changes, so that it can pass the data back up in its original form.

Before I talk about what each layer actually does, I would like to reiterate that the selection of functionality at each layer is basically arbitrary. There are those who would argue that it would have been better to combine the top three layers into one or to divide the data link layer into two. Technology changes, networks change, and it is difficult to foresee where the focus will be years later. But this is the model, and one way or another it has always been made to work.

It is useful to understand what these calls actually look like and what data they pass to each other. In their simplest form, the calls and data structures look like Figure 2-3. The call from one layer to another occurs at a SAP. (You might have wanted to call it an interface, but ISO does not appreciate common terms. Instead we use acronyms wherever possible.) There is a SAP between each layer, and it defines which entity in the service (lower) layer is being accessed by the calling (upper) layer. So, it is the point at which the service is accessed.

One of the calls the SAP can make is to transfer a block of data. This block has no meaning to the service layer. It is just a unit of data so many bytes long. We call it a service data unit (SDU). At each layer,

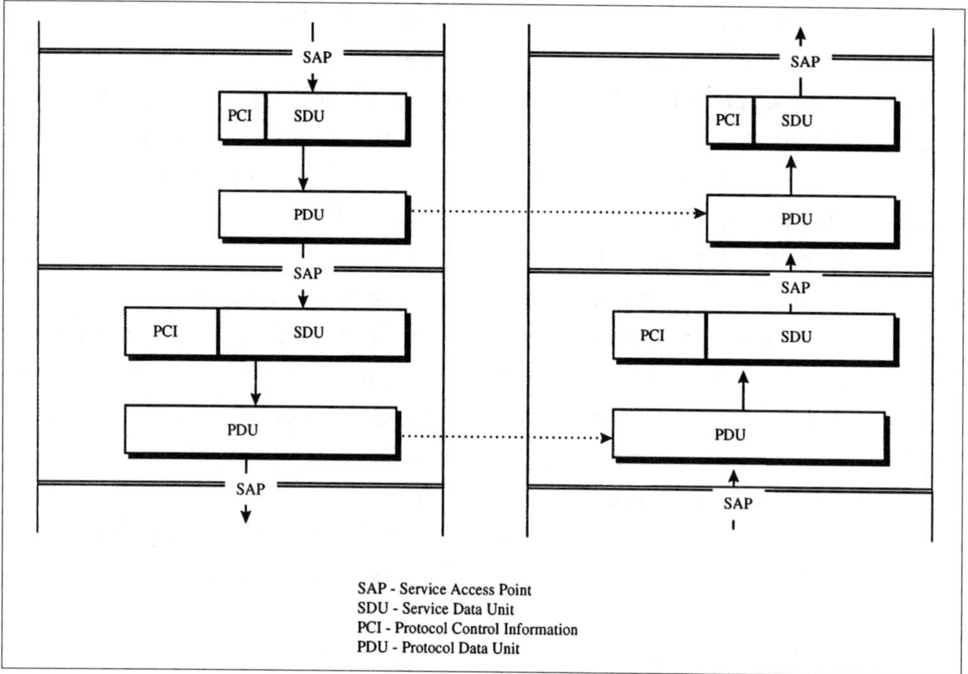

Figure 2-3. *SAPs and PDUs*

we need to perform some operations on the data, and unless we are performing compression we end up with more information than we started with.

The difference in data is usually appended to the SDU and is called the protocol control information (PCI). Together they form our PDU, which is what our peer expects on the other end and will convert back into the original SDU to pass back up to the caller.

On the outbound side, the appending is repeated at each level until we reach the physical layer, which transmits the data to the other node. There the control information is stripped at each level, until it reaches the application layer with the same data the source application sent.

So far I have made it sound like the only calls one network module makes to another are to transfer data (SDUs or PDUs, depending on how you look at it). Actually, there are a number of different types

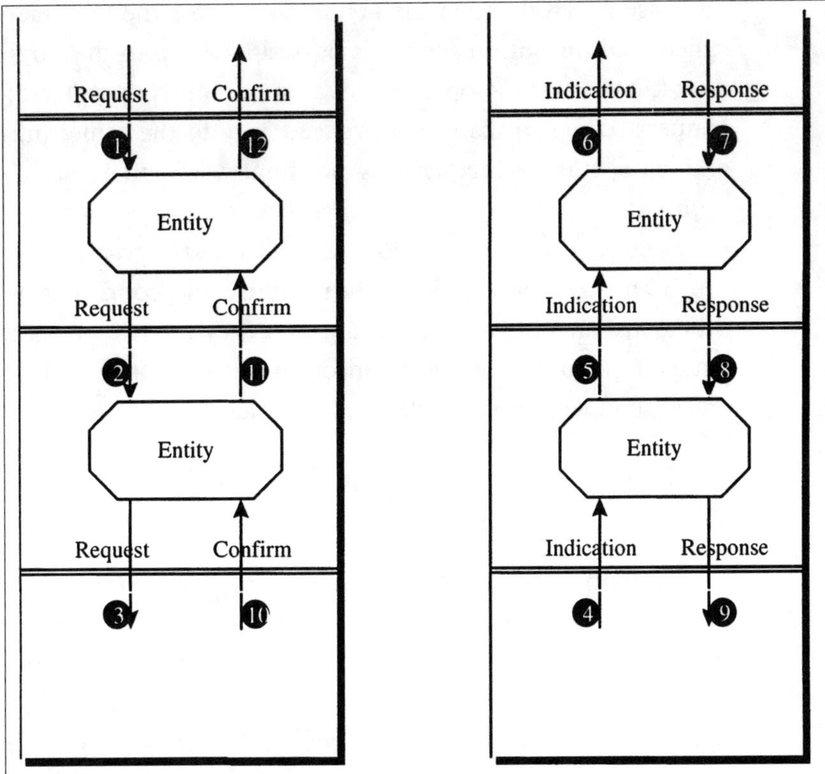

Figure 2-4. *Service Primitives*

of calls you can make from one layer to the other. Often you want to set up a connection, transfer data and then close the connection. For each of these three, and for other operations, the OSI model defines a set of four actions, called service primitives.

In Figure 2-4 you see these primitives at work. To communicate from one layer entity to its peer on a different node, it calls the layer below it with a request. This request is passed down to the physical layer and across the physical line. At the other end the request is transformed into an indication. Each layer passes the indication back up until it reaches the top.

In some cases the operation may be complete at this point. However, usually it requires a confirmation. So the recipient sends a response down through the layers and across the line. Here it is now called a confirmation, and it is passed back up to the originator, who now knows that the operation was successfully completed. If it was a connect request, it can now proceed and do the same thing with several data transfer requests. And finally, it can issue a disconnect request.

Some actions are considered confirmed services and require all four events (request, indication, response and confirmation), whereas others are unconfirmed, meaning that they require only the first two. An example of confirmed connections and unconfirmed data transfer and disconnection using the OSI notation would be:

```
CONNECT.request      CONNECT.indication     CONNECT.response   CONNECT.confirm
DATA.request         DATA.indication
DISCONNECT.request   DISCONNECT.indication
```

I will now give a short overview of the individual OSI layers. Note that this is only very superficial. You can look into the references at the end of the chapter for more details on any of the layers. In addition to a synopsis of the layer's functionality, I will highlight some points that you are likely to encounter when dealing with electronic mail.

Physical Layer

The physical layer, shown in Figure 2-5, is different from all the others in that it is the only one that actually communicates directly with its peer. It is at this level that the actual connection between two computers is described. So this layer needs to describe the physical characteristics of the medium of transmission (kind of wire or fiber-optic cable), as well as the electrical characteristics of the transmission.

Figure 2-5. *Physical Layer*

Some of the specifications at the physical layer include:

- **Voltage levels**: What are the minimum and maximum voltages; what are considered 1 and 0?
- **Carrier frequency**: Often the medium does not support digital signals. Then it needs to be sent using an analog signal at some specific frequency.
- **Data transmission rate**: How many bits can be transmitted per second?
- **Type of modulation** (frequency, frequency shift keying, phase, amplitude): How is the data encoded on the carrier frequency?
- **Type of multiplexing** (frequency division, wavelength division, time division): How can we transmit several signals at the same time over the same physical medium?

Data Link Layer

The data link layer, as shown in Figure 2-6, calls on the physical layer to perform the actual transmission. It is actually one of the most complex layers, but fortunately, we do not need to know too much about how it operates to be able to use it. Some of its functions include:

- **Flow control**: It ensures that the sender does not send faster than the receiver can process. If it has the capacity to send faster, it either reduces the rate or waits between transmissions until the receiver can catch up.

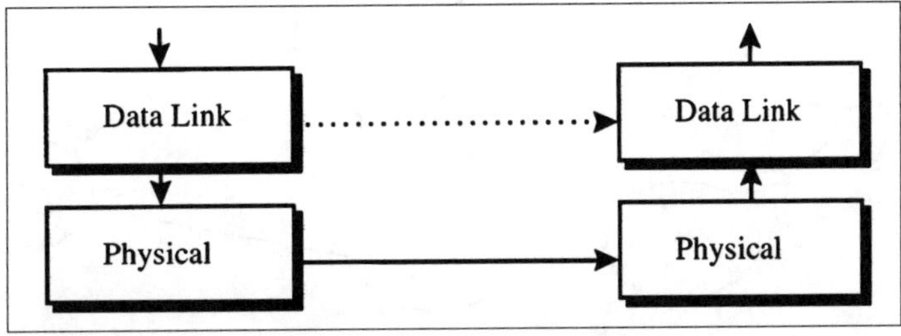

Figure 2-6. *Data Link Layer*

- **Framing:** The data (which might be very long bit streams) is broken into segments called "frames." Each frame can receive control information such as a checksum to ensure that it is transmitted correctly.
- **Error detection and correction:** Based on the control information sent with each frame, it is possible to tell when an error in transmission has occurred. Some times it is even possible to determine what the error was and correct it. Otherwise, it requests that the frame be resent.
- **Media access:** Often several machines share one physical medium between them (ethernet, token ring or airwaves). There needs to be some mechanism for them to negotiate who is transmitting when.

Note that this last point—media access control—is conceptually different from the others and also quite involved in terms of implementation. Because of this, you often hear people talking about the data link layer actually consisting of two layers: the data link layer proper and the media access control (MAC) layer.

Network Layer

The network layer is responsible for routing packets from the source to the destination. It needs to know the topology of the network in order to find an optimal path across which to transmit the data so

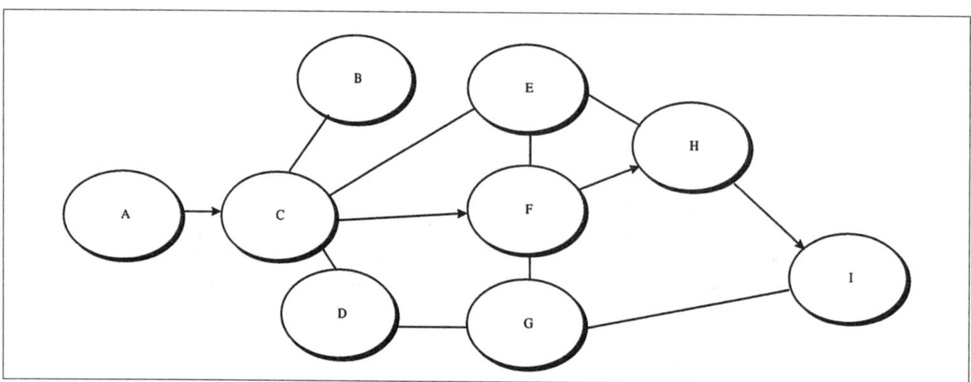

Figure 2-7. *Routing a Packet from Node A to Node I*

that it arrives quickly and efficiently. When there is congestion along one path in the network, or when one of its links fails, it needs to adapt its routing to a new optimal path.

Consider a topology as shown in Figure 2-7, where a user on node A sends a message to someone on node I. There are quite a number of paths the data could take (A=>C=>E=>F=>G=>I or A=>C=>D=>G=>I, or even A=>C=>D=>G=>F=>E=>C=>D=>G=>F=>E=>C=>D=>G=>I, if we allow it to visit the same nodes more than once). Clearly, not all of the possible paths are equally efficient, and it is the job of the network layer to find a short path that is not already overloaded. On each node the network layer must find the adjacent node, which is next along the best path, and forward the packet in that direction.

It is important to realize that we cannot tell which path is optimal simply from looking at a diagram. We need more information. For example, we need to know how fast each of the links is, and how saturated they are. The network layer has access to this information, and using some networking algorithms, it is able to find the best path.

With that in mind we can take a look at the example. The network layer on node A has a trivial task. It only has one connection, so it doesn't take much calculating to figure out that it should send the packet on to node C. Here the choice becomes more difficult though. It can now forward the packet to one of the nodes D, E or F. Let's say it chooses F. It now has C, E, G and H as possibilities. It should be able to exclude C since that is where it just came from, but it will have to employ a best-path algorithm to determine which of the other two to choose. At node H the decision is fairly simple again, since it has a direct connection to the target node, I.

As you can see from Figure 2-8, we cannot effectively represent the network layer with only two machines. The layer gets its name from the fact that it is the first layer (from the bottom up) having to do with a network, as opposed to simply a connected system.

The network layer will really be sending two types of data out to its peers. It has to pass the same user data that all the other layers pass between the systems, but it also needs to send routing data between the network layers. How else will all the nodes in the network know

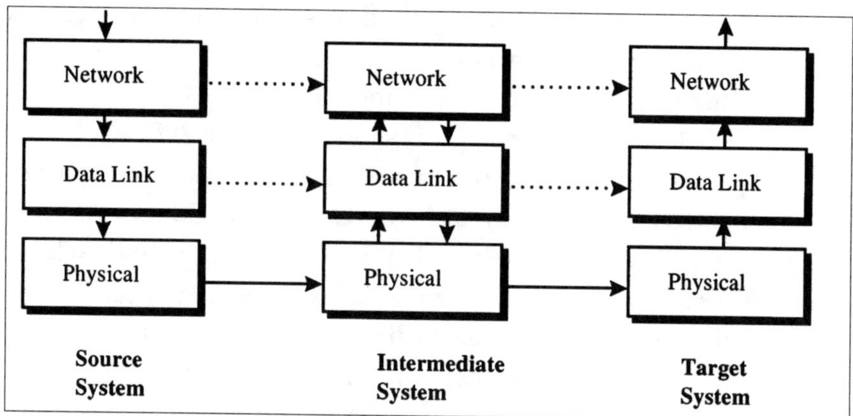

Figure 2-8. *Network Layer*

when one link has gone down or another is saturated? They have to keep their routing tables up to date.

Like all the other layers, the network layer can receive requests to transfer information from the layer above it (the transport layer). It also receives indications from the layer below it (the data link layer) that data has arrived. With the incoming data, it first has to check whether it is destined for this node, in which case it can pass the data up to the transport layer with an indication. Otherwise, the incoming data becomes outgoing data, and the network layer needs to look up the next node and request to the data link layer to send the packet on in that direction.

Connectionless or Connection-Oriented Service?

No technology is without its internal debates, and networking is no exception. People have argued about every aspect of it. But there is one topic that has caused more discussion than any of the others, and that is the question of connection-oriented network service (CONS) versus connectionless network service (CLNS). The issue is whether or not a connection should be established for each communication and data should be transmitted through that connection, or whether it would be better to send the data and rely on the application to determine whether the data was transmitted correctly.

You could compare these two approaches to engaging in a phone conversation and sending a letter with the postal service. When you want to talk on the phone with someone, you have to wait for a connection. Then you know that the data you are transmitting (i.e., what you are saying) is being received at the other end. It is always possible that you will lose the connection, but if that happens, you will usually be notified by a dial tone. Traditionally, you will have a circuit from your phone to the phone at the other end, and everything you say will pass through that channel. You also know that what you say will be heard in the order in which you say it.

When you send a letter, you have no idea whether or when it will arrive. If you send several letters, they may go through different central post offices and arrive out of sequence. You could have an agreement with your correspondents, though, that you will number your letters and they will order them and send you back replies periodically, letting you know which ones have or have not arrived.

A phone conversation is like a connection-oriented service, whereas sending a letter is like a connectionless service. Some of the points in favor of a connection-oriented service are that the calling application needs to do less work if it can rely on the data and that it may also be more efficient to pass large amounts of data through an allocated pipe than to route each piece of data individually. On the other hand, to argue in favor of a connectionless service, it is questionable whether it is possible to provide a completely error-free service, so maybe the application should decide whether it wishes to check the data itself.

While I just explained the debate in terms of an application and the networking service to keep it simple, in reality, it is the various layers of the OSI stack that can implement a connection-oriented or connectionless service to their callers. To a large extent, the choice at each layer is independent of the choice in the others. The transport layer would typically have the same operation as the layers above it, but it might call a network layer component of the other camp. At the data link layer you might, again, have an implementation of either connectionless or connection-oriented service.

These combinations are feasible. In practice, however, the only layer anyone cares about in this debate is the network layer. The transport layer almost always provides reliable service. It can call on either a connectionless network (and do more work) or a connection-oriented network (and do less work but be dependent on the network). Almost everyone has gone in favor of connectionless service. DECnet has traditionally been CLNS, and IP (Internet protocol) has always been CLNS. The main notable exception is X.25, which is still in widespread use and offers connection-oriented service.

X.25

X.25 never established itself completely outside of Europe, and even there the Internet is conquering the market with the result that X.25 is slowly disappearing. Not fast enough for my taste, though, as I find it unnecessarily cumbersome for the value it provides. But, alas, it will be around for a few more years, and, since X.400 is often used in conjunction with it, I should discuss it here.

Actually, X.25 is not only a network layer, but really occupies the bottom *three* layers of the OSI stack. The third layer is where it most distinguishes itself, though, and is the point where its services can be accessed.

The standard defines a connection-oriented network service across a (usually public) packet-switched data network (PSDN). We know what CONS is. What about a PSDN? "Packet-switched" means that the data is segmented into manageable "packets" (usually of a maximum size of 128 bytes) and transferred across the network. These packets do not necessarily all travel along the same path. The circuit may switch from packet to packet. Nevertheless, the service provider undertakes to deliver all of the packets error-free and in the order in which they were sent.

Let's take a first look at the X.25 model.

In Figure 2-9 you can see a simple representation of the X.25 model. It consists of systems falling into three categories. The PSDN, usually provided by the country's Postal, Telephone and Telegraph (PTT) authority, includes external interfaces called data circuit-terminating

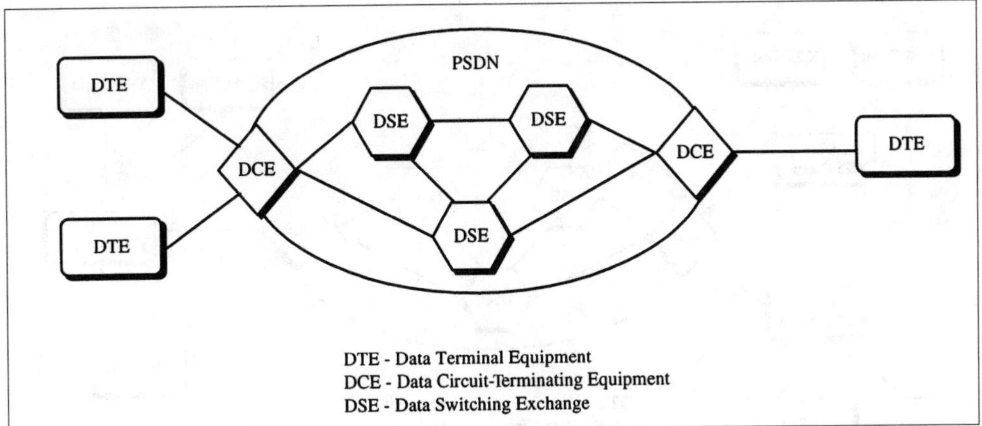

Figure 2-9. *X.25 Model*

equipment (DCEs) and internal routers called data switching exchanges (DSEs). The customer must have DTE (data terminal equipment) to access the PSDN and communicate with other DTE. The PSDN connects to a DCE and requests a circuit to the remote DTE. The interface between the DTE and DCE is the only part in this model that concerns X.25. The protocols within the PSDN (i.e., between DSEs) are up to the service provider to define and implement internally. Since they affect nobody else, there is no standard interface.

The model in Figure 2-9 is fine as long as we have only one computer that needs to connect across the PSDN. If we have only one machine, or at least only one with X.25 related applications, then this will be sufficient. But often we have several systems that we would like to connect to the outside. We could request circuits for each of them and give each a direct connection to the PTT. But that may not be the most cost-effective solution.

In Figure 2-10 we see another alternative. We can define one system as the interface to the PSDN. We can call it the gateway. On the other systems, we just need to install some software to allow us to be able to get to the X.25 modules in the gateway. Basically, we are tricking the PSDN, although in no malicious way. It thinks that the DTE is the end system, but we can get the DTE to relay the information between our actual client and the PSDN. For a detailed explanation

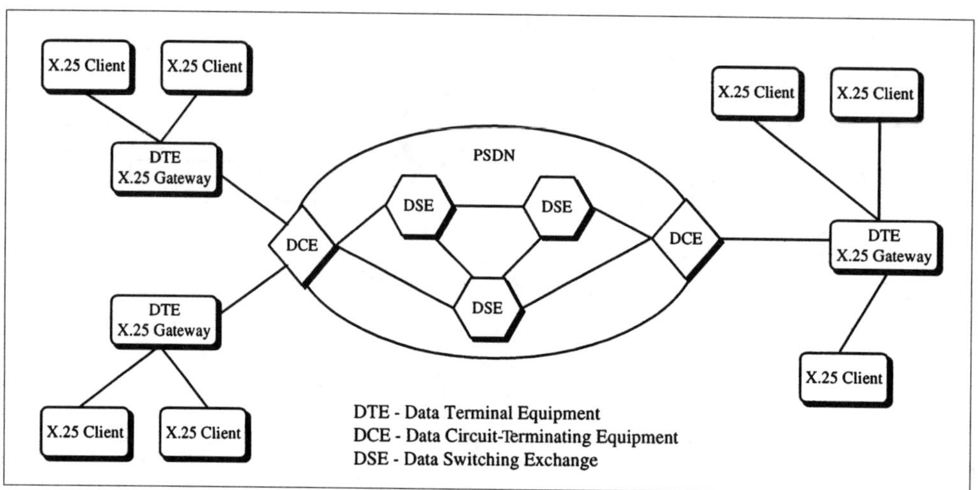

Figure 2-10. *Extended X.25 Model*

of the way that the X.25 functionality is accessed by applications, see Martin and Leben (1992), chapter 18.

That is almost it with regard to X.25. The rest can be left to the network specialists. But there is one point you may still be interested in knowing, since you won't get very far without it. How do you tell your DCE with which DTE you want to connect? I am sure you can guess that each DTE must have a unique address, and that the service provider gives this to you. These addresses have a specific format that even has its own standard (X.121) to describe it. A DTE address consists of a string of a maximum of 15 digits. The first four digits identify the PSDN and the last two are a subaddress that is optional and can be used by the DTEs for further identification (to select one of the non-gateway nodes, for example). The PSDN provider assigns the digits in between to your DTE.

Network Addresses

Network addresses identify the node in a network of machines running OSI protocols. In OSI terminology, we call the address the NSAP (network service access point) and, in characteristic OSI style, it has been designed to be very flexible. Its main requirement is that it be unique, and verifiably so. It does not have to be user-friendly, and it is not. It can be up to 40 decimal digits long and is composed of three fields (see Table 2-1). The first is called the authority and format identifier (AFI) and identifies the type of address. The second is the initial domain identifier (IDI) and the third is the domain specific part (DSP). The term initial domain part (IDP) is also used to designate the AFI together with the IDI.

Table 2-1. *OSI Network Address*

IDP		
AFI	IDI	DSP
49	-null-	00-30:AA-00-04-00-1F-C1:21

As the name implies, the AFI indicates both the authority that allocates the IDIs and the format of the IDIs. It also specifies whether the DSP is decimal or binary. The AFIs are assigned to different authorities by both ISO and ITU, using different schemes. One common AFI you will see is 49, which indicates that the IDI is null and the entire address is therefore contained in the DSP. These addresses are assigned locally by organizations that do not have a need to maintain direct OSI connections outside their boundaries and therefore need to have unique addresses only within the company. They are relieved of the need to request a unique address from an authority.

Transport Layer

At the transport layer, our job is to ensure a certain level in the quality of service. How easy or difficult this is depends on two points. The job is a lot easier if not much is expected of us from the session layer above than if we have stringent demands put on us. And at the other end, if we can depend on the network layer to give us everything we need, we obviously have a much easier job than if we have to do it ourselves.

The demands made on us are basically good performance (short delays and high throughput) and few errors. We will leave it up to the

OSI model and the implemented protocols to decide how to accomplish this, but we do need to be aware of the fact that OSI defines a transport protocol (TP) that it divides into five classes, as shown in Table 2-2.

Table 2-2. *Transport Protocol Classes*

TP0	Basic class
TP1	Basic error recovery class
TP2	Multiplexing class
TP3	Error recovery and multiplexing class
TP4	Error detection and recovery class

TP1 and TP3 are rarely used. TP0 is a basic class that assumes the underlying network is error-free and does not provide any error recovery. You obviously cannot use this very well in a connectionless network unless you don't care about your data arriving. In a connection-oriented network this would work fine, since the network layer is already ensuring that no errors are passed.

TP2 is similar, but it allows you to combine multiple transport connections over the same network connection, which is useful if you want to save money and your transport connections are not fully utilizing the network. Here again, you have no error detection so you cannot operate across a connectionless network layer.

TP4 provides full error detection and recovery. This provides reliable connections over an unreliable network. In the case of a connectionless network, this is the class most often used. You could also run it across a connection-oriented network, in which case the error detection at the transport layer would be quite trivial.

Session Layer

The session layer is not a particularly sophisticated one at the present time. Its main tasks are to allow the upper layers to establish sessions and to provide certain defined session services. For example, one of the most commonly mentioned services is checkpoints. If you are copying a file from one node to another, you can ask the session layer to periodically establish checkpoints. If the copy should fail for any reason, you will then only need to restart at the latest checkpoint rather than reissue the entire copy operation.

Presentation Layer

The presentation layer offers services relating to the format of the data transmitted. For example, it can give you the opportunity to encrypt or compress data or to convert it from ASCII to EBCDIC or any other format. But even though it can work with different formats, there is one that stands above all others. We will see it in conjunction with X.400, but it applies equally well to other OSI and ITU networking protocols.

X.400 uses a binary form to store messages and all other data it processes. It is a terse format, and all X.400 components must conform to it. This concise representation has its advantage. It is optimized for efficiency. While it may be possible to tweak it here and there, you won't find a lot of redundant data lying around.

On the other hand, it also has its disadvantages. It is not human-readable. If you take a look at the binary dump of the data, you will most likely not be able to guess what you are looking at. If you get a corrupt message, you will have your work cut out for you trying to repair it.

Be that as it may, we don't have an option, so if you have X.400, you will be using X.400's format. It is often called ASN.1 (ISO 8824), meaning "abstract syntax notation one," or the first attempt at an abstract syntax notation. Actually, though, the format is defined by what are called the basic encoding rules (ISO 8825), which are an implementation of ASN.1 and are used in conjunction with it.

If this sounds logical to you, you are a prime candidate for one of the ISO committees. For the others, let me see if I can paint you a clearer picture. When any networking component transfers data from one system to another, it is usually data about some objects. A mailing system like X.400 might, for example, be transferring a body of a message or an addressee. For each of these objects there are three syntaxes to describe the data that defines the object's attributes:

- Abstract syntax
- Local syntax
- Transfer syntax

ASN.1 is used for the abstract syntax. Not surprisingly, the others are called concrete syntaxes. The difference is that an abstract syntax does not concern itself with the actual storage of the data. If it says something is an integer, it does not matter whether it is stored in 1's complement or 2's complement, whether it uses one byte or ten bytes of storage, or how the bytes are ordered. These details are considered concrete, and the abstract syntax wants nothing to do with them.

This higher-level notation has the advantage that it is not encumbered by any technical restrictions. Numbers can be indefinitely large and strings indefinitely long. It is wholly impartial with regard to any particular implementation, so it does not favor operating systems with particular storage formats. In fact, it would be great if we could just use the abstract notation for everything.

The problem is that the abstract notation, by itself, is useless. When we store data, we have to store it in a particular format. We have to take a position in the debate of big endian *versus* little endian and select 1's complement or 2's complement. Fortunately, the data we store locally is really nobody's concern but our own. As long as our code is the only program to touch and read the data, we can choose any format we like. This is called the local syntax, and ISO is happy to give its blessing to any local syntax that works.

Unfortunately, we still have a problem. Networking modules generally have to work with modules on other systems, which may have different implementations. I am sure you will agree that it simply will not do to have a program sending a four-byte integer to a counterpart that is expecting a two-byte integer. So we have to define an implementation for any data that is sent across the network. And this transfer syntax must, of course, be identical for all networking components.

This is what is specified by the basic encoding rules. They take each atomic data type, give it a tag, and pass the tag, its length, and its value in a specific pre-defined format. Some people also call this TLV encoding, referring to the three parts.

I am sure you are keen on seeing an example of this format, so here is one to satisfy your curiosity, although hopefully you will never have the need to look into the format of X.400's data structures in depth.

At first glance the syntax does not look too bad. We have a few definitions written in so-called Backus-Naur form (BNF), which is often used to define the syntax of programming languages:

```
InformationObject ::= CHOICE {
        ipm      [0]     IPM,
        ipn      [1]     IPN }
IPM ::= SEQUENCE {
        heading          Heading,
        body             Body }
Heading ::= SET
this-IPM                         ThisIPMField,
originator               [0]     OrignatorField OPTIONAL,
authorizing-users        [1]     AuthorizingUsersField OPTIONAL,
primary-recipients       [2]     PrimaryRecipientsField DEFAULT [[,
copy-recipients          [3]     CopyRecipientsField DEFAULT [[,
blind-copy-recipients    [4]     BlindCopyRecipientsField OPTIONAL,
replied-to-IPM           [5]     RepliedToIPMField OPTIONAL,
obsoleted-IPMs           [6]     ObsoletedIPMsField DEFAULT [[,
related-IPMs             [7]     RelatedIPMsField OPTIONAL,
subject                  [8]     EXPLICIT SubjectField OPTIONAL,
expiry-time              [9]     ExpiryTimeField OPTIONAL,
reply-time               [10]    ReplyTimeField OPTIONAL,
reply-recipients         [11]    ReplyRecipientsField OPTIONAL,
importance               [12]    ImportanceField DEFAULT normal,
sensitivity              [13]    SensitivityField OPTIONAL,
auto-forwarded           [14]    AutoforwardedField OPTIONAL,
extensions               [15]    ExtensionsField DEFAULT {}}
...
Expiry-TimeField ::= Time
Reply-TimeField ::= Time
ImportanceField ::== ENUMERATED {
        low     (0),
                normal  (1),
                high    (2) }
...
```

Really the syntax is quite straightforward. You start at some presumably top-level object and see what its components are. Then you look each of them up and trace the structure down until you get to the atomic types. At that point, you would need to look up the encoding rules to see how they should be stored or transferred.

Quite simple. There is one small problem, though. There are a lot of syntax definitions. In fact, the tomes of protocol specifications are full of them. An object may have a dozen levels in the hierarchy of its syntax tree, and you might have to apply a thousand rules to arrive at the final representation. While it would be great fun to work it out in your head, some network developers are very unexciting people and have instead written compilers that read in ASN.1 specifications and generate code for them to produce and read data.

PSAP

When dealing with X.400 and X.500 you will often need to specify a presentation service access point (PSAP). This is how you let an MTA (message transfer agent) or DSA (directory system agent) connect with its peers. Most network applications do this by having you indicate the network address of the remote node, and that is essentially what the PSAP is.

The PSAP contains the NSAP, which is the OSI equivalent of a network address. But since there may be several presentation-level entities (i.e., several applications) and the architecture wants to allow you to use multiple stacks, you need to specify selectors for each of the intermediate layers. These are called:

- **PSEL**: Presentation layer selector
- **SSEL**: Session layer selector
- **TSEL**: Transport layer selector

In most cases you will use the same name for each of the selectors. So the PSAP for your DSA might be:

```
"DSA"/"DSA"/"DSA"/nsap
```

When you declare your local DSA, you register it with this PSAP, and remote DSAs can access it provided they know the PSAP.

Application Layer

The application layer is where all of the actual user and system applications reside. This is where any user interaction should take place, and it is the express purpose of all the other layers to make life at the application layer as easy as possible.

X.400 is one example of a module that resides in this layer. Others include FTAM (file transfer, access, and management) for file transfer, and virtual terminals to facilitate logging into remote hosts.

TCP/IP

History of the Internet

Before delving into the protocols that make up what we now consider the Internet, I will give you a sketchy background of how this beast came into being. Some time ago, in the late 1960s to be more exact, the U.S. Department of Defense funded an agency called the Advanced Research Projects Agency (ARPA). They involved a few universities in the idea of connecting their computers together.

At the time, there were no protocols in use for data communications, so the participants in the project had to create their own. From them we have the precursors of TCP and IP, which are now the most prevalent protocols in the industry. The network created by ARPA was called ARPANET, and it was a fairly loosely controlled set of computers that were connected together.

The successor to ARPA, DARPA (Defense Advanced Research Projects Agency) decided that it was not secure to have civilian and military machines on the same network. So they pulled their sites into a separate network called MILNET and left the remaining participants to work on their own under the auspices of the Internet Advisory Board (IAB). The IAB now oversees the work of the Internet Research Task Force (IRTF) and the Internet Engineering Task Force (IETF).

Internet Protocol

The primary protocol we talk about in the Internet world is the Internet protocol (IP). In the OSI model it would be classified as a network-level protocol, since it takes care of routing packets from one IP system to another.

An IP address falls into one of four classes: A, B, C and D. You are unlikely to hear much about class D, which defines multicast addresses, but the classes A, B, and C are frequently mentioned. In each, the address consists of four bytes, but the meaning attached to the various bytes differs. The addressing scheme assumes that there will be a given number of networks (meaning private networks of the various participating organizations) and a given number of computers (hosts) in each network.

We could say that we would use the first two bytes to determine the organization and the second two bytes to designate the computer. That would mean we could have 2^{16} or 65,536 networks with each 65,536 hosts. But that could cause a problem for large companies like Microsoft or IBM that might have more than 65,536 hosts attached.

So we could take the approach of using only one byte to designate the organization and the other three to designate the host. However, we would then run into the limitation of being able to accommodate only 2^8 or 256 networks. It would also be wasteful since small companies with just a handful of hosts would be allocated 2^{24} (or millions) of addresses.

In order to maximize the use of the four bytes, the competent authorities decided to make the length of the network and host addresses variable. This way, small companies would not need to use up much address space, and large companies could still have the blocks of addresses they required.

The actual division into the three classes is arbitrary. The addresses probably could have been allocated more efficiently, but there is only so much that can be done with 32 bits, and it is not always easy to foresee how the industry will evolve.

If you take a look at Table 2-3, you can see how the three classes allocate the addresses. In a class A address the first bit must be 0, and the seven bits following it designate the network. In the example this would mean that the network was 42 and the host address in the network is 123.123.123.

Table 2-3. *IP Address*

Class	Byte 1	Byte 2	Byte 3	Byte 4	Example
A	0NNN NNNN	HHHH HHHH	HHHH HHHH	HHHH HHHH	42.123.123.123
B	10NN NNNN	NNNN NNNN	HHHH HHHH	HHHH HHHH	133.111.222.333
C	110N NNNN	NNNN NNNN	NNNN NNNN	HHHH HHHH	200.123.123.123

N-bit specifies network address
H-bit specifies host address (within network)

As you can imagine, class A addresses were in high demand and soon ran out. The companies that were fortunate enough to receive them can run networks with 2^{24} addresses, which is enough for any organization in the foreseeable future.

But there are many more than 128 companies[1], so some had to settle for the next best thing. In the class B address, we have 1 followed by a 0 and a 14-bit network designation. In the example, this would mean that the network was 133.111 and the host address 222.333. The companies that requested and received class B addresses generally are not too badly off either. Most of them can function on 2^{16} or 65,536 addresses.

Alas, we are also coming to an end in the set of 2^{14} or 16,384 class B network designations. It may seem like a large number, but there are many more companies than that in the world, and now everyone wants to make sure they are not left stranded.

So we have moved on to class C. In the example, this would mean a network address of 200.123.123 and a host address of 123. The local addresses have only 8 bits (2^8 or 256 addresses) in this scheme. This can be very limiting, and in many cases it means that organizations are required to request several class C blocks in order to accommodate all of their users.

You can guess the next problem. The class C addresses are running out, too. That doesn't leave us much room for maneuvering.

[1] To be picky, it would be 126 companies, since both 0 and 127 are reserved.

Fortunately, the issue is not yet acute. We still have a few years, according to current projections, but clearly this problem needs to be resolved.

But rest assured, the network designers of the Internet have not been sleeping and saw the problem coming years ago. It may have taken some time to come to an agreement on how to resolve the bottleneck, but the consensus is that IPv6 will provide enough addresses for many years to come.[2]

Subnets

A central theme to IP is the concept of a subnet. What does that mean? Let's start with the fact that IP is a routable protocol. Unlike NetBEUI, for example, this means that you can connect to machines that are not on your own local area network (LAN). A device called a router will pass your requests and responses from one subnet to another, making it possible for machines on both to communicate with each other.

In order to do this, we need to indicate the IP address of this router (called the default gateway) and let the networking components know which addresses are on our own LAN and which need to pass through the gateway. There are a number of different ways we could tackle the problem, but in the IP world the subnet mask has won out.

With four bytes we are able to say who is local and who is on the other side of the gateway. Basically, we compare the remote address with our local address and see where the differences lie. Then we see if any of the different bits are in the subnet mask. If so, we need to go via the gateway. Otherwise, we can stay on the LAN.

---

2 Briefly, IPv6 increases the IP address size from 32 bits, to 128 bits thereby greatly expanding its addressing capabilities. It also simplifies the header format, improves support for extensions and options, adds flow labeling capability (e.g., for real-time service) and supports authentication and privacy capabilities. Further discussion of IPv6 is beyond the scope of this book, but if you are interested in IP, you may care to reference RFC 1883.

So let's say my IP address is `16.158.96.168` and I have a subnet mask of `255.255.255.0`. If I want a connection to `16.158.96.200`, will I need to go through the gateway? To be thorough we should convert the addresses to binary form:

Table 2-4. *Subnets and Subnet Masks*

	Decimal	Binary Form
Source IP Address	16.158.96.168	00010000 10101110 01100000 10101000
Destination IP Address	16.158.96.200	00010000 10101110 01100000 11001000
Difference		00000000 00000000 00000000 01100000
Subnet Mask	255.255.255.0	11111111 11111111 11111111 00000000

As you can see in Table 2-4, there are only two different bits in the two IP addresses, and they are not set in the subnet mask. This means that we do not need to use the gateway.

If our connection is to `17.158.96.168`, we have a different situation. Only one bit is different (the last bit in the first byte). However, this bit is set in the subnet mask, so we do need to pass through the gateway.

One final point on subnets: Don't confuse them with the network address classes discussed in the previous section. The network is an architectural construct without immediate technical ramifications. The subnet is a technical product of the network topology. I will express it by way of an example: If a company has no internal routers, then it may very well be that the subnet mask matches the network bits in the address. In any case, the subnet should always include those bits as a minimum. But it may be that an organization has several subnets within its network. In that case, the subnet mask (as in the example above) would extend beyond the network selection.

Transmission Control Protocol

IP is a connectionless network protocol. As we saw in the discussion on OSI, this means that it sends packets to its destination without ever checking whether they arrive intact and in sequence or, in fact, whether they arrive at all.

For some applications this is all right, but for many (including electronic mail), it is insufficient. So we have another layer that does all of the checking to ensure we have a reliable connection between the two systems. In the OSI model we would situate the transmission control protocol (TCP) at the transport layer. TCP is a connection-oriented protocol. Its current definition was specified in 1981 in RFC 793 to provide a standard mechanism for reliable transmission across the Internet. Close to the same time (1980), a connectionless transport level protocol was also defined on IP. UDP (user datagram protocol) was specified in RFC 768 and is widely used, although not for mail-related functions.

Some of the tasks of TCP include:

- Flow control
- Resequencing
- Acknowledgment
- Multiplexing

To perform these tasks TCP calls on its network protocol, which is usually IP, although it need not be. It is possible to run TCP over OSI or other stacks, though this is rarely done.

Addresses, Ports and Sockets

When applications talk to each other in the TCP world, they do so through sockets. The idea is that all networked applications have sockets through which they can send and receive data. Rather than the program having to worry about all the underlying networks, it just opens a socket in its counterpart and reads and writes data as if to a file.

What is a socket? Very simply, it is an IP address and a port number. We have already talked about the addresses in the previous sections, but let's take a look at the ports. Similar to the PSAP discussed earlier in the OSI section, the port allows us to uniquely address an application in the network.

Every process that wants to make use of TCP needs to request a port number. For a lot of the standard applications there are already predefined port numbers published in RFCs.

Internet Assigned Numbers Authority (IANA) has divided the port numbers into three ranges: the well-known ports (0–1023), the registered ports (1024–49151), and the dynamic and/or private ports (49152–65535). The first are controlled and assigned by IANA. The second are not controlled by IANA but are registered with them as a service to the Internet community. The last range is entirely for private use.

Some of the most frequently used port numbers are listed in Table 2-5:

Table 2-5. *TCP Port Numbers*

Port Number	Application
21	FTP
23	TELNET
25	SMTP
53	Domain (i.e. DNS)
70	Gopher
102	ISO Transport Services
109	POP2
110	POP3
143	IMAP, IMAP2, IMAP 4
144	News (NNTP)
220	IMAP3
389	LDAP

In addition to specifying the TCP port number, we also need to ensure that the target IP system realizes that the incoming packets are for TCP and not some other protocol. At the IP level, our system therefore records the TCP protocol number in the packets.

There are a number of other protocols that can be layered on top of IP. You can see some of the most common in Table 2-6.[3]

[3] A more complete list of IP protocol numbers, as well as TCP and UDP ports, is listed in RFC 1700 or, more up to date, in:

```
ftp://ftp.isi.edu/in-notes/iana/assignments/protocol-numbers
ftp://ftp.isi.edu/in-notes/iana/assignments/port-numbers
```

Table 2-6. *IP Procotol Numbers*

Number	Protocol
1	ICMP — Internet Control Message Protocol
6	TCP — Transmission Control Protocol
8	EGP — Exterior Gateway Protocol
17	UDP — User Datagram Protocol

Since there can be only one application per port, the combination of network address, protocol number and port number allows us to identify any registered process on the network.

Domain Name System

Four-byte addresses are no problem for computers to understand. They are concise and provide all that the networking layer needs to know to identify the route to the next computer.

For humans they are less than ideal. Some people are better with numbers than others, but everyone I know can remember mnemonic names better than twelve semi-random digits. Clearly there was a need to allow end-users to enter mnemonic names that could be translated by the application or networking software into numeric Internet addresses.

Initially a file called "hosts" did this. It had an entry for every computer on the network and its corresponding IP address. The network would look into the file and convert from human-readable to machine-readable form when making network connections.

The key phrase in the above paragraph is "for every computer on the network." When there were only a handful of computers connected, this was no problem. But as the network started to grow—and grow rapidly—this solution became impossible to sustain. It wasn't feasible to coordinate the updates and replicate the file throughout the network in a systematic and efficient manner.

So domains were born. And with them came the domain name system (DNS). Rather than having one central file that was modified, every domain maintained its own set of hosts and resolved the address translations for any requests made on names in its domain.

Domains

I will come back to how this resolution occurs in a moment, but first let us look at the domains themselves.

Domains are arranged hierarchically. There is one domain called the root, which is quite simply a dot. All other domains are subordinate to it. At the top level is a fixed set of domains. In a mnemonic Internet address this will be the right-most component. Some of the most common top-level domains include:

- **com**: Commercial organizations
- **gov**: Government departments
- **mil**: Military
- **edu**: Educational facilities
- **net**: Networks
- **org**: Usually nonprofit organizations
- any of the ISO country codes, such as:
  - **at**: Austria
  - **ie**: Ireland
  - **my**: Malaysia

Underneath this top level, the list is much more open-ended, although it is still necessary to register in order to prevent name clashes.

If I take as an example the name of my server, `mcps2.msa.dec.com`, we can tell that it resides in the domain `msa.dec.com` which, in turn, is part of domain `dec.com`, a subdomain of the top-level domain `com`. The full host name is also referred to as the FQDN or full-qualified domain name.

In Figure 2-11 you can see the hierarchy for the domain structure of `mcps2`.

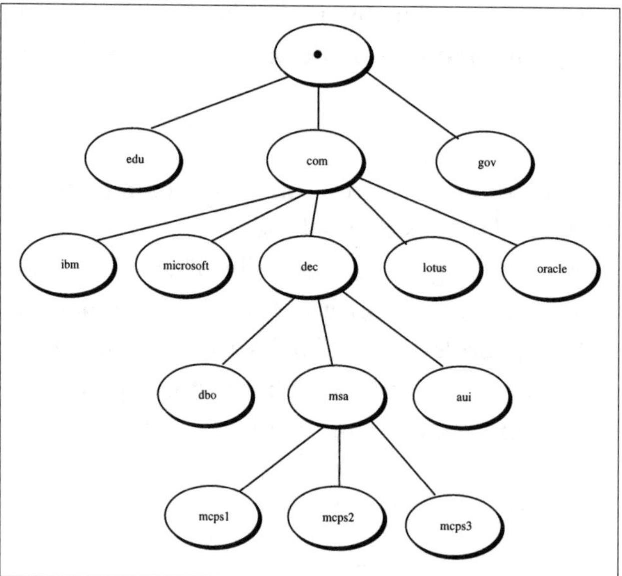

Figure 2-11. *DNS Domain Hierarchy*

NAME RESOLUTION

With a domain name system we have a way of compartmentalizing the whole network into small areas. This gives us several advantages:

1. It gives us an idea of where a particular machine in the network might be.
2. We can ensure that no two systems on the network have the same name.
3. It ensures that every machine in the network is known to us; if not directly, then at least indirectly.

The last point is less obvious than the first two and depends on the cooperation of the systems involved. The way it works is illustrated in Figure 2-12. Whenever a client (called name requestor) needs information about a given resource (e.g., the IP address of a given host), it makes a request to a piece of software called a name resolver. The resolver then takes care of finding the information on the Internet. It will have a default name server from which it will first request the

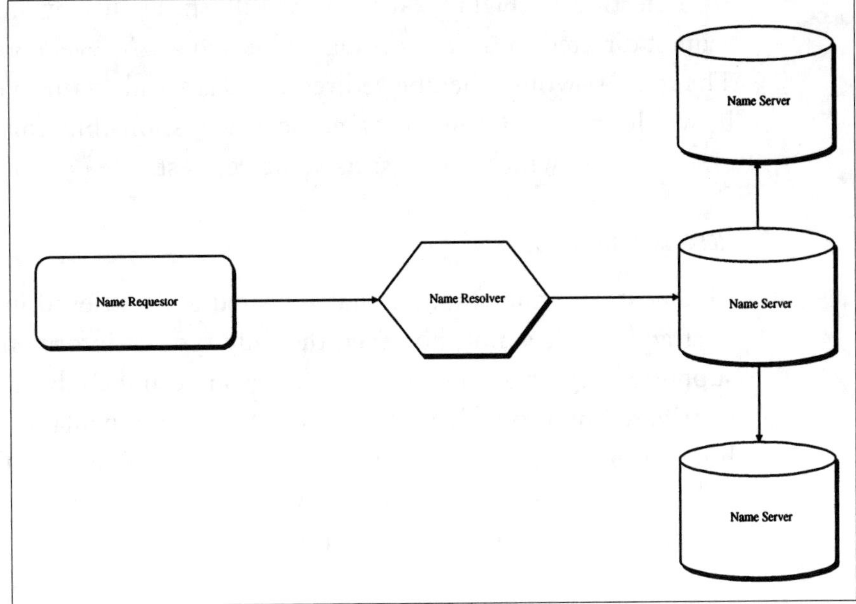

Figure 2-12. *Name Resolution*

information. If that server has the data locally, it will return it to the resolver, which passes it on to the requestor.

However, if the server has not cached the information, it will simply provide the name of another server to the requestor. This process will be repeated until the request is satisfied. If all the name servers in the Internet are connected to each other, this should work satisfactorily. At least it will if we implement the scheme correctly. Otherwise, we could have infinite loops of redirection at worst, and highly random redirection at best.

The idea is to take advantage of the hierarchical scheme and only redirect name servers in the right direction. To understand this you need to be aware of the fact that name servers are assigned zones of authority. A zone is essentially a subtree for which the server is responsible. I might have a server, `ns1` responsible for the zone `mcps1.msa.dec.com` and another, `ns2` for `msa.dec.com` with exception to `mcps1.msa.dec.com` and still another for `ns3` `dec.com` with exception to `msa.dec.com`.

Referring to Figure 2-12 we can illustrate this by imagining a request directed to `ns1` for a resource located at `exchange.microsoft.com`. The request would then be redirected to `ns2` and again to `ns3`. There it would need to find a name server responsible for the zone `microsoft.com`, which could satisfy the request.

Resource Records

The most common resource that is stored and retrieved in DNS is a host address. It is not, however, the only type of information that is supported. Quite a number of other resources take advantage of the distributed nature of DNS to make information available across the Internet. The most common types of record are listed in Table 2-7.

Of particular interest to us will be the mail exchange (MX) records, used for routing mail across domains.

Table 2-7. *Common Resource Record Types*

Type	Meaning
A	Host address
NS	Name server
CNAME	Canonical name
SOA	Start of authority
WKS	Well-known services
MX	Mail exchange

DNS entries are structured with five fields (see Table 2-8). They are identified by a domain name, which is followed by the time-to-live. This tells the DNS servers how long to cache the entry when they retrieve it. (If this is not specified, the server will keep the cached value indefinitely and will not be aware of changes made to the domain.) The class is almost always IN, since DNS has been closely tied to the Internet. In theory, another network could also implement DNS and provide a completely different set of resource records, but this is not likely to happen. The type indicates what type of resource we are describing (e.g., A, NS, MX), and according to the type, we may also store some additional data.

Table 2-8. *Structure of Resource Record*

Domain name	Time-to-live (seconds)	Class (IN)	Type	Data (depending on type)
lotus.com	100000	IN	A	
lotus.com	100000	IN	MX	20 lotus2.lotus.com

```
nslookup
> set type=a
> Server: msagps.msa.dec.com
Address: 16.157.64.33

Name: lotus.com
Address: 192.233.136.1
> set type=mx
> Server: msagps.msa.dec.com
Address: 16.157.64.33

lotus.com          MX preference = 20, mail exchanger = lotus2.lotus.com
lotus.com          MX preference = 10, mail exchanger = lotus.com

lotus.com          nameserver = NIC.NEAR.NET
lotus.com          nameserver = BU.EDU
lotus.com          nameserver = NOC.CERF.NET
lotus2.lotus.com   internet address = 192.233.136.8
lotus.com          internet address = 192.233.136.1
NIC.NEAR.NET       internet address = 192.52.71.4
BU.EDU             internet address = 128.197.27.7
NOC.CERF.NET       internet address = 192.153.156.22
>
```

Figure 2-13. *Example of Looking Up DNS Records*

Highlights

- Both TCP/IP and OSI networks are routable and are not limited to LANs.
- The addressing scheme of OSI allows for unlimited growth in the foreseeable future. IP will run out of addresses in the next few years and will need to be migrated to IPv6.
- IP is closely related to DNS, a universal and comprehensive scheme of naming hosts. OSI is not bound to any naming service, and there is no internationally accepted authority for administering one.

- Both OSI and IP offer connectionless network service. OSI also offers connection-oriented network service, but demand for it is decreasing.
- Connections in IP are made to a socket, which is an address, plus a protocol selector (e.g., TCP or UDP) and a port number. OSI connections are made to applications by specifying the address plus transport selector, session selector and presentation selector.
- OSI protocols typically use ASN.1 encoding to transfer data between systems. IP protocols often use text data, but for more complex interaction many are also now using binary form.

References

For a complete (technical, but very readable) look at how networks are implemented, see:

Tanenbaum, Andrew S. 1996. *Computer Networks.* Englewood Cliffs, N.J.: Prentice Hall. ISBN 0-13-394248-1.

For a thorough examination of Digital's implementation of the OSI model:

Martin, James, and Joe Leben. 1992. *DECnet Phase V: An OSI Implementation.* Boston: Digital Press. ISBN 1-5558-076-9.

For an evaluation of a number of different network implementations:

Fortino, Andres, and Jerry Golick. 1996. *Multivendor Networking.* New York: McGraw-Hill.

For a thorough description of TCP/IP:

Black, Ulysses. 1995. *TCP/IP & Related Protocols.* New York: McGraw-Hill. ISBN 0-07-113296-1.

For an overview of TCP/IP administration from a Unix perspective:

Hung, Craig. 1992. *TCP/IP Network Administration.* Sebastopol, CA: O'Reilly and Associates, Inc. ISBN 0-93175-82-X.

For a description of DNS and its most popular implementation, BIND:

Albitz, Paul, and C. Liu. 1992. *DNS and BIND*. Sebastopol, CA: O'Reilly & Associates, Inc. ISBN 1-56592-010-4.

And the network-related RFCs:

Deering, S., and R. Hinden. 1995. *Internet Protocol, Version 6 (IPv6)* (RFC 1883).

ISI USC. 1981. *Internet Protocol* (RFC 791).

ISI USC. 1981. *Transmission Control Protocol* (RFC 793).

Mockapetris, P. 1983. *Domain Names—Concepts and Facilities* (RFC 882).

Mockapetris, P. 1983. *Domain Names—Implementation and Specification* (RFC 883).

Postel, J. 1980. *User Datagram Protocol (RFC 768).*

Rose, M. T., and D. E. Cass. 1987. *ISO Transport Service on top of the TCP* (RFC 1006).

Reynolds, J., and J. Postel. 1994. *Assigned Numbers* (RFC 1700).

Chapter 3

Message Structure

The primary function of a mail system is to deliver messages from one user to another. Before discussing how the transfer works, it is good to understand what data we are actually working with. The OSI and Internet formats are quite different, but they do offer analogous contents.

X.400 Message Structure

P2 versus *P22*

There are not many differences between the 1984 and 1988 X.400 standards, but there is one that is impossible to miss. The structure of the messages is different. The implication of this is that if an MTA (message transfer agent) sends a message encoded with the 1988 standard to an MTA that was implemented using the 1984 standard, the message will not be accepted.

In 1984 the name P2 was given to the protocol for user agents to speak to each other, and it defines the structure of a message. In 1988 it was extended, and the new protocol was baptized as P22. It is important to realize that 1984 MTAs do not understand P22, so it is necessary for 1988 MTAs to know if their connection is with a 1984 MTA. If so it can send the message in P2 format.

Message Types

The unit of communication between two MTAs is an MPDU (message protocol data unit). When one user sends a message to others, we call it an interpersonal message (IPM). The bulk of the MPDUs are IPMs, but there are also other kinds.

Reports

Reports are notifications that are returned to the originator when the message has been routed to its final destination. They indicate whether or not the delivery of the message was successful. If the message arrives at the recipient's user agent and the UA recognizes the recipient, the delivery is considered successful and the notification is called a delivery report. On the other hand, if there are any problems with the routing, or if the user agent does not accept the message, the delivery is considered unsuccessful and the notification is called a nondelivery report.

Delivery reports are not usually requested, since users expect their messages to get through and do not want to be burdened by countless notifications of success. It is generally much more convenient to assume success and act only when a nondelivery report arrives.

For exceptions to this and elaboration on the two kinds of notification (delivery and receipt), see Chapter 1, under "Message Attributes."

Probes

Probes are essentially empty messages that are sent to test whether a message can be delivered to a particular recipient. The probe is passed to an MTA, which will route it on until it gets to the delivering MTA. It is never actually delivered, though. Instead, a report is issued telling the originator that the probe was successful. If, on the other hand, it cannot be routed or delivered, a nondelivery report is issued.

Interpersonal Message Structure

As Figure 3-1 shows, an interpersonal message can be divided into an envelope and a content. The envelope contains the information used by the MTAs to route the message to its destination. They don't care about

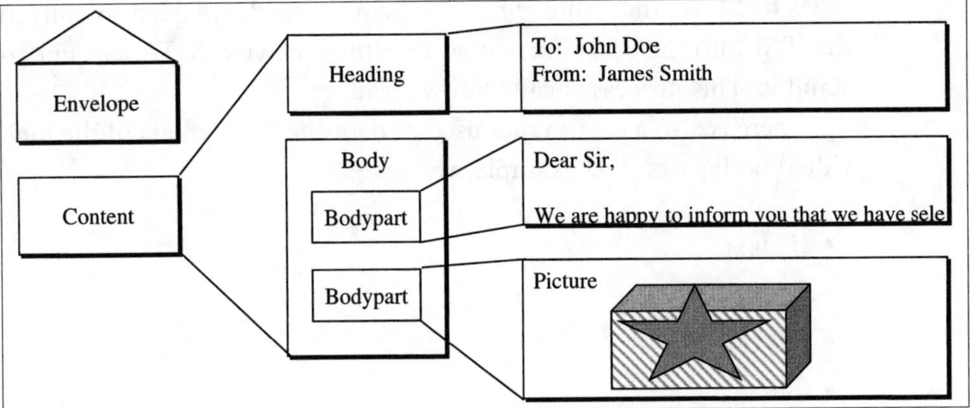

Figure 3-1. *IPM Structure*

what the message contains and do not read it. The envelope has all the information they need. The content can be further subdivided into a header and a body. The header is what you would typically imagine at the head of a letter: information about the author, recipients and date of writing. The body is all the actual information that is being sent to the destination. It can be one or more bodyparts (also called attachments).

Interpersonal Message Content Types

Interpersonal messages can be further subclassified by content type. There are only seven content types that refer to the entire message:

- Any content type
- Unidentified
- Electronic data interchange
- IPMS 1984
- IPMS 1992 — externally defined
- IPMS 1992 — file transfer
- IPMS 1992 — passthrough

If we receive a 1984 IPM, it is not a big problem for any X.400 MTA. But we need to make sure that we don't send 1988 or 1992

IPMs to MTAs that cannot handle them. Instead, we need to convert the IPM into the 1984 format so that the receiving MTA can understand it. This process is called downgrading.

There is also a set of types used to describe the formats of the individual bodyparts. For example, we have:

- IA5Text
- T.61
- ISO Latin
- ODIF
- Bilaterally defined
- Externally defined

This is one of the most problematic areas of X.400. There are a large number of types of bodyparts, and no single UA is able to understand all of them. So what can we do about sending incomprehensible bodyparts to a particular user? Some solutions are:

- Convert the bodypart to a format understood by the recipient's UA.
- Return the message to the sender with an indication of why it could not be delivered.
- Allow the unconverted message to pass through to the user, who can then decide what to do with it (ignore it, or extract it and view or print it with other software)

We will return to conversion later in the chapter.

Internet Message Structures

The structure of Internet messages was originally defined in RFC 561, years before SMTP came into being. At that time it was customary to copy messages to their destination as simple files, using FTP (file transfer protocol). This obviously had the disadvantage that it is difficult to tell by looking at a file who it is from and to whom it is directed. So in 1973, an Internet message structure was defined to contain some header fields and the body of the text.

This structure was later refined in RFCs 680, 724, and 733 before reaching the current standard, 822. It is now assumed to be used in conjunction with RFC 821, although the two are independent of each other. RFC 821 describes how to transfer the file, while RFC 822 describes how it is structured.

Each header line consists of a field name (terminated by a colon) followed by a field body. The field body usually fits on one line, but if it is too long, it can span multiple lines. Each continuation line just needs to begin with a space. When all the header fields have been entered a null line (two consecutive line breaks) indicates that the message body follows.

There are only a few fields required to make the message valid. It must contain a creation time, source and destination, as seen in Table 3-1.

Table 3-1. *RFC 822 Header Fields*

Required fields	
Field Name	**Description**
Date:	Creation time of the message
From:	Originator ("source") of the message
To: or Bcc:	Recipient ("destination") of the message

Optional fields	
Field Name	**Description**
Received:	Provides tracing information
Subject:	Subject of the message
Reply-to:	Preferred address of originator
Return-path:	Return address

The list indicated in the RFC is open; in other words, it is possible for applications or other standards (e.g., MIME, as we shall soon see) to include additional fields. They need only to adhere to the header-line syntax rules and avoid clashing field names with other standards and applications.

If we look at the message below we can see some of the fields discussed. The required fields ("Date," "To" and "From") are there, as well as the "Subject" and several "Received" fields. One thing to point out is that they are added to the message content as it passes from one MTA to another. This implies that the message that arrives at the recipient does not have exactly the same content as that sent by the originator.

These fields allow us to see how the message was transferred through the mail system. We can see which MTAs routed it, as well as when they forwarded the message. In the example, we can see that the message was routed from `mts.dec.com` to `dasmts.imc.das.dec.com` to `mcpserver.msa.dec.com`. If we look at the times, we can also see how much time it spent at each server. Be careful to take into account the time-zone offsets.

The message came from a message router system ("MR-Received") through the PMDF gateway into SMTP. After the "Received" fields we see a number of lines appended by PMDF to retain the Message Router parameters.

We can also find some fields that are related to MIME (e.g., "Content-type").

```
Received: from dasmts.imc.das.dec.com by mcpserver.msa.dec.com with
 SMTP (Microsoft Exchange Internet Mail Service Version 5.0.1389.3)
 id FXVSFPBB; Sun, 9 Mar 1997 18:52:16 +0800
Received: from mts.dec.com by dasmts.imc.das.dec.com
 (PMDF V5.0-7#16470)
 id <01IGADL50QCG00VJX2@dasmts.imc.das.dec.com> for
 John.Rhoton@mcpserver.msa.dec.com; Sun, 09 Mar 1997 05:51:46 -0500
 (EST)
Received: with PMDF-MR; Mon, 10 Mar 1997 02:43:44 +0000 (GMT)
MR-Received: by mta MSAM00; Relayed; Mon, 10 Mar 1997 02:43:44
+0000
MR-Received: by mta ZPOM00; Relayed; Sun, 09 Mar 1997 10:51:06
+0000
MR-Received: by mta DASMTS; Relayed; Sun, 09 Mar 1997 10:51:45
+0000
Alternate-recipient: prohibited
Disclose-recipients: prohibited
Date: Sun, 09 Mar 1997 10:42:00 +0000 (GMT)
From: JOHN RHOTON <"JOHN RHOTON"@A1.MSAM00.MSA.mts.dec.com>
Subject: I: A short RFC 822 Message 1
To: John Rhoton - Exchange <John.Rhoton@mcpserver.msa.dec.com>
Message-id: <01IGADL5MFLI00VJX2@mts.dec.com>
```

```
MIME-version: 1.0
Content-type: TEXT/PLAIN; CHARSET=US-ASCII
Content-transfer-encoding: 7BIT
Posting-date: Sun, 09 Mar 1997 10:43:00 +0000 (GMT)
Importance: high
Priority: urgent
X400-MTS-identifier: [;44342001307991/882035@MSAVC]
A1-type: MAIL
Hop-count: 3

This is a short one-line message —John
.
```

Seven-Bit ASCII

When mail first started on the Internet, the only thing people sent each other was text. And since the Internet started in the U.S., where the whole alphabet and set of standard punctuation characters can fit into the 128 (2^7) possible combinations of seven bits, it seemed logical to use the eighth bit as a parity bit. That gave it some extra redundancy, which can never be a bad thing.

The first 128 characters defined by the ASCII (American Standard Code for Information Interchange) character set define the 26 characters of the English alphabet in upper and lower case and most of the characters you would encounter in everyday use. Text that uses only the first 128 ASCII characters, encoded in seven bits, with one parity bit added on, is termed seven-bit ASCII.

Uuencode

But there are a lot more than 128 characters in the various international alphabets. ASCII defines 256, which accommodates most European alphabets.[1] This gives us characters like à, ø, ñ, ∂, and symbols like ¥ or §. Since we don't really need a parity bit anyhow (there is enough error checking elsewhere), we might as well use all eight bits in the byte to be able to offer the maximum number of characters to our mail users.

---

[1] The discussion of various (mostly Asian) multi-octet character sets is beyond the scope of this book. Unicode is one such mechanism, that has gained popular support and is included in Windows NT.

There is a problem, though, when it comes to SMTP. The protocol doesn't permit the use of the eighth bit. This means that, even if you write an SMTP MTA that passes eight bit characters, they will be lost on the journey to their recipients.

What we need is a way of fitting eight bits into seven. And of course we need to preserve the eight bits so that we can retrieve them at the other end. That may sound like an impossible task; bits do not compress very well. But if we do not mind adding a few extra bytes, we can come up with a workable solution.

Think of it this way: You have seven bytes, each with eight bits of data. If you line them up sequentially and pack seven bits each into another set of bytes, you can fit the same data into eight seven-bit bytes. This is essentially what we need to do to accommodate an eight-bit character set in the seven bits that SMTP will recognize.

Unix systems have a utility, which has since been ported to all major operating systems, that does just that. It is called "uuencode" and packs a file with eight-bit data into another with seven-bit data so that it can be transmitted across seven-bit channels like SMTP. At the other end, the user can invoke its counterpart called, unsurprisingly, "uudecode."

Of course, these days we no longer have only the issue of international characters. Most people are no longer sending much plain text at all to each other. Instead, we have data files used by a wide variety of PC applications. And most of these, regardless of the language, store their data in eight bits, making something like uuencode, or MIME, indispensable.

MIME

What is MIME (multipurpose Internet mail extension)? We already have a way to send any format of file across the Internet. What more could we want?

We want a lot. It is nice to be able to send any type of file, but what if we want to send more than one file at once? And while we're at it, wouldn't it be nice if the recipient didn't have to know what kind of file we were sending? It would be great if the system just knew it was an Excel spreadsheet and launched the application without any intervention.

In short, there are two issues that need to be addressed. The first is the definition of various content types, which may be binary. And the second is the ability to encapsulate multiple files into one message.

These issues were originally solved independently in two RFCs. RFC 934 dealt with the question of encapsulation, while RFC 1049 defined content types for the bodyparts. These two standards were later combined, refined and renamed. Currently, RFCs 2045–2049 define MIME and are considered to be one single standard.

How does MIME work? Essentially, the structure of a multipart MIME message is that it concatenates all of the attachments with separators between them. Each bodypart will indicate what type of file it represents by specifying a content type. In addition, it will indicate how this file is encoded for transfer through the mail system.

Content types are composed of a top-level media type plus a subtype. While both top-level types and subtypes are defined in the standard (RFC 2046), it is possible to freely define additional types and subtypes; for example, to accommodate proprietary word-processor formats.

As seen in Table 3-2 there are five discrete top-level types that describe contents corresponding to single files. There are also two composite top-level types that may encapsulate discrete or other composite contents.

Table 3-2. *Top-Level Media Types*

Media Type		Subtypes
Discrete	text	plain, richtext, enriched
	image	jpeg, gif
	audio	basic
	video	mpeg
	application	octet-stream, PostScript
Composite	multipart	mixed
	message	rfc822

In addition to specifying the content type, we can also indicate how the data is encoded. Bear in mind that these formats often require eight-bits per byte and that SMTP only supports seven. So there is clearly a need to do some transformation.

Table 3-3 lists the mechanisms for encoding that are defined by the MIME standard. Encoding is somewhat of an overstatement for the first three on the list. Seven-bit, eight-bit and binary simply leave the data as it is. Their distinction is therefore only semantic. Quoted-printable and base64, on the other hand, actually reduce eight-bit data to seven-bit form for transfer through the network.

Table 3-3. *Content Transfer Encoding*

Mechanism
7-bit
8-bit
binary
quoted-printable
base64

The choice of which mechanism to use depends largely on the data being transferred. If it is true binary data, then base64, as we will see in a later section, is most suitable. Using this mechanism to specify all eight-bit characters (128–255 in the collating sequence) will ensure that only seven-bit characters are stored in the message.

You will notice that the following example begins by indicating the content type:

```
Content-Type: multipart/mixed; boundary="---- =_NextPart_000_01BBFFD3.8ACB9240"
```

This is an indication that the message is composed of multiple bodyparts of different types (mixed). It tells us that the boundary between bodyparts will be `"---- =_NextPart_000_01BBFFD3.8ACB9240"`. Why use something so cryptic? It needn't be that extreme, but we do need to ensure that the separator is not contained in any of the bodyparts themselves. That means that this separator should ideally also be unique, to avoid problems if MIME messages are embedded as attachments to other messages.

Now that we have sorted out the structure, we can look for the first bodypart by searching for the separator:

```
------ =_NextPart_000_01BBFFD3.8ACB9240
Content-Type: text/plain; charset="us-ascii"
Content-Transfer-Encoding: 7bit
```

It tells us the first bodypart is plain text using US-ASCII, which can be (and is) encoded in seven bits (i.e., not encoded). The next attachment is after the next boundary:

```
------ =_NextPart_000_01BBFFD3.8ACB9240
Content-Type: application/msword; name="x.doc"
Content-Transfer-Encoding: base64
```

We have a Microsoft Word document, originally stored in the file X.DOC. In order to transfer the binary data across a seven-bit channel (SMTP), it has been encoded using the base64 encoding scheme.

```
------ =_NextPart_000_01BBFFD3.8ACB9240
Content-Type: application/octet-stream; name="y.xls"
Content-Transfer-Encoding: base64
```

Our last attachment is a Microsoft Excel spreadsheet, although the sending mail application did not know this. It just tells us that it is a stream of bytes. Fortunately, we have the file extension and a little background knowledge of the Microsoft Office suite.

There is one more separator to let us know when we have come to the end of the spreadsheet.

```
------ =_NextPart_000_01BBFFD3.8ACB924--
```

Quoted-Printable

Quoted-printable is useful for packaging eight-bit text in seven bits. All of the seven-bit characters (the first 128 in the collating sequence) can be represented in their natural form. For most text, this will be the vast majority of the characters. The syntax also allows characters to be represented by an "equals" sign followed by the (ASCII) hexadecimal value of the character (e.g., "=FF" can be used to represent a binary 255).

This encoding is useful for transferring natural-language text with only occasional eight-bit characters. A typical binary file would have 50 percent eight-bit characters, each of which requires three characters to store. This means that it would double (50%+3*50% = 200%) the size of the file. A text file with only, for example 5 percent eight-bit characters requires only 10 percent additional (95%+3*5% = 110%) storage.

In addition, we can take into consideration that, in the absence of a decoding mechanism, text that has been encoded using quoted-printable is still largely readable. Due to the high ratio, binary text would be confusing to decipher, but then again, it is usually difficult to read anyhow.

Base64

Base64 lends itself to true binary data. Since it consistently requires 33 percent overhead, it is better than quoted-printable for random binary data (high ratio of eight-bit to seven-bit characters) but worse for text (low ratio). Also, as opposed to quoted-printable, it is never easily decipherable. Base64 receives its name from the fact that its encoding uses 64 characters (A–Z, a–z, 0–9, +, /), each requiring six bits (2^6=64).

The algorithm works as follows:

1. Take three bytes (24 bits) of binary input data
2. Divide the bits into four groups of 6 bits
3. Encode each group into one base64 character
4. You have four printable output bytes
5. Go back to step 1 for some more data

As an example, let's take three bytes of binary data:

```
Decimal:      127 167 16
Hexadecimal:  3F A7 10
Binary:       0011 1111 1010 0111 0001 0000
Regrouped:    001111 111010 011100 010000
              31     58     28     16
Base64:       P      6      c      Q
```

Our result, "P6cQ," is shorter than if we had just included the ASCII version of the decimal or even hexadecimal notation (four characters *versus* eight or six), but it is still not as compact as the binary source, which only had three bytes. The benefit of the 33 percent overhead is that we can analyze the result much more easily and can transmit it across many more connections.

Bodypart Formats and Conversion

X.400 Message Conversion

When the message processor determines the next routing step of a message, it has three options:

1. Send the message on without conversion;
2. Convert the message and send it on;
3. Return the message to the sender.

It decides which of these is appropriate according the following three criteria:

1. Instructions in the envelope of the message;
2. Content types and encoded information types listed for the recipient;
3. Converters available.

Let's look at this process in more detail.

Bodypart Types

There are a number of different ways you could categorize the types of formats you might want to include in an electronic message. By far the most common would be text. But what exactly is text?

To represent text we could use any number of encoding schemes, the most popular of which is ASCII. But even with ASCII we had two important variants: seven-bit and eight-bit ASCII. Encoding the data in seven bits meant that you had an extra bit to use for parity, but it also meant that you could only represent

2^7=128 characters. With eight bits, on the other hand you could represent 2^8=256 characters.

For many English-speaking users, 128 was largely sufficient, as they could represent all 26 characters of the alphabet in upper and lower case, as well as numerals and punctuation marks. But many of the five billion people living outside the English-speaking countries were frustrated by the fact that characters in their languages were not included in the character set. As a result, many European users preferred eight-bit ASCII, which accommodated a large number of the European characters.

Even a set of 256 characters cannot be all-inclusive, however. There was obviously a need for a specification that addressed the needs of all the languages, particularly the Asian ones, which have a much larger array of characters. And there have been such specifications, which usually require two or four bytes per character and are able to fulfill the needs of all the languages in the world.

On the other hand, it seems somewhat inefficient to be using four-byte characters if I am writing a message in English, where one byte would do. It would be nice to be able to choose the character set we need when we need it.

This is essentially the approach of many of the specifications. You can use one set of characters and alternate to others as needed. Often this is called shifting. You shift one set of characters in and another out. How the binary values in your data are mapped to particular characters depends on the mode you are in (i.e., which character set is currently shifted in).

And now for some of the character sets in X.400:

IA5 International Alphabet Five. This is similar to seven-bit ASCII. It can't do much, but it has the advantage that virtually everyone can understand it. It has been around since 1984.

T.61/ISO6937 Teletex characters. Supports essentially the same as eight-bit ASCII, but is encoded in either one or two bytes (accent and characters separate). It is therefore more complex than IA5.

ISO8859 ISO Latin. Set of single-byte character sets that support the major European languages.

GeneralText ISO 10021 defines a bodypart type that is a wrapper for any number of component character sets. Each announces itself at the beginning (and is included in the EITs, or encoded information types, for the bodypart) and can be called upon in the text. GeneralText was not defined in 1984 but is the preferred text format for a 1988 IPM.

These are for text files, but we also have countless other types of files, anywhere from those used by PC applications to binary data files. How can we transmit them across a mail backbone? Actually, the transmission is easy, but how will the recipient (or his software) know what the data is? The answer is that we need to tag it somehow.

A 1984 MTA only recognizes a very limited number of different bodyparts. If you want to send something else, you have only one option. You can send it as a bilaterally defined bodypart, meaning that you and the receiver have made arrangements for a particular type and both know what is being transmitted. If you need a generic solution, you are on your own.

In 1988 this was recognized as a problem and a new bodypart type, called "externally defined," was defined. With this you could indicate an encoded information type with the bodypart, and the recipient's UA/MTA could look it up and process the bodyparts accordingly. This made it possible to send and receive an unlimited number of bodypart types. Each just needed an officially recognized EIT, and everyone would be able to process it. This solution has worked reasonably well, even though not all vendors registered their formats and consequently the EITs for some bodyparts are not universally recognized.

In 1992 another extension was made to the X.400 specification, adding another type of content to a regular 1992 IPM. It is one that permits file transfer bodyparts. An FTBP does not have an associated EIT, but rather a file specification. At present, the main user of FTBPs is Microsoft Exchange.

Routing and Conversion

Let us look again at what happens when the message processor examines a message for a particular recipient. Besides the routing instruction for the O/R (originator/recipient) address it will also see a list of content types and encoded information types that the user (or set of users if it is a partial O/R address) can understand.

The message processor can look into the envelope of the message to see if these match. If they do, then all is well and the message will go on to the recipient(s). But if they do not match, then the message processor will need to do something about the discrepancy. The first action is to check if the message allows conversion at all. This is one of the flags specified by the originator and found in the envelope. If we can't convert, then we need to send the message back to the originator with an indication that the message could not be delivered as requested.

If the message can be converted, the next step is to find the converters. The MTA should have a list of converters. It selects one with the source type found in the document and tries to find a target type that would be acceptable to the recipient. If it finds none, we are back to sending a nondelivery notification, but if it is successful, we can send the message onward with the converted bodypart.

Note a couple points about the converters. First, the list of EITs for an O/R address is ordered. This means that if two conversions are possible to make the bodypart recognizable, the MTA will choose the first. Second, converters may be lossy or not. "Lossy" means that they lose information during the conversion. If you convert a plain text document to a word processor format it will probably not lose any data (i.e., the text will be preserved), so it is not lossy. On the other hand, the conversion in the other direction will likely lose data (fonts, colors, graphics), so it is considered lossy. A converter that is not lossy is always preferable to one that is lossy.

SMTP and Conversion

The Internet targets a world where everyone has PCs. As such, it does not offer any means for the backbone to automatically convert mail messages—how would the backbone know what software a user has on his or her PC? Rather than take the chance of converting messages and losing some of the information, the Internet standards focus on ensuring that there are universal (MIME) tags that identify the format of the bodyparts. The user's software can then take care of converting for viewing the incoming mail messages.

This approach has the obvious disadvantage that the user may have a PC without the required software (or even a character-cell terminal) that cannot do anything with the received format. It would be possible to build the conversion capabilities into the hosts receiving the mail, but the Internet standards do not address the issue.

Highlights

- X.400 1984 supports structured messages using a predefined set of formats.
- X.400 1988 allows external definition of formats of bodyparts.
- SMTP allows only unstructured seven-bit text messages.
- With MIME user agents, it is possible to encode structured messages composed of text and binary bodyparts.
- MIME contains printable text that can be decoded with relative ease.
- X.400 uses ASN.1 encoding, which is not printable and is more difficult to decode.
- Both quoted-printable and base64 encoding require substantial overhead compared to the minimal overhead necessary for ASN.1 encoding.

References

For more information on the RFCs, see:

Alvestrand, H. 1993. *Equivalences Between 1988 X.400 and RFC-822 Message Bodies* (RFC 1494).

Alvestrand, H., et al. 1993. *Mapping Between X.400 and RFC-822 Message Bodies* (RFC 1495).

Alvestrand, H. 1993. *X.400 Use of Extended Character Sets* (RFC 1502).

Crocker, D. 1982. *Standard for the Format of ARPA Internet Text Messages* (RFC 822).

Freed, N., and N. Borenstein. 1996. *Multipurpose Internet Mail Extensions (MIME) Part One: Format of Internet Message Bodies* (RFC 2045).

Freed, N., and N. Borenstein. 1996. *Multipurpose Internet Mail Extensions (MIME) Part Two: Media Types* (RFC 2046).

Freed, N., and N. Borenstein. 1996. *Multipurpose Internet Mail Extensions (MIME) Part Three: Message Header Extensions for Non-ASCII Text* (RFC 2047).

Freed, N., and N. Borenstein. 1996. *Multipurpose Internet Mail Extensions (MIME) Four: Part Registration Procedures* (RFC 2048).

Freed, N., and N. Borenstein. 1996. *Multipurpose Internet Mail Extensions (MIME) Five: Part Conformance Criteria and Examples* (RFC 2049).

For a short introduction to the X.400 architecture for electronic mail, see:

Radicati, S. 1992. *Electronic Mail: An Introduction to the X.400 Message Handling Standards*. New York: McGraw-Hill. ISBN 0-07-051104-7.

Chapter 4

Backbone Topology

Addressing

The topology of a mail backbone may be represented by the addressing scheme it uses. However, this is not a necessary component of the addressing mechanism. In fact, it is rarely desirable to have the address linked to the topology; it simplifies the task of routing but creates a dependency on the backbone, which the user should not directly see.

It may be easiest to illustrate this with an example of paper mail. If I send a message to my sister in California, I address the letter to "Sharon Rhoton, street address, Ventura, CA, postal code, U.S.A." I do not need to attempt to determine which route the letter will follow and include all the intermediate destinations, as in "local post office -> Central Vienna post office -> New York -> Los Angeles -> Ventura -> Sharon Rhoton." And yet that is the way many electronic mailing systems used to work. With Digital's Message Router, you need to enter all the intermediate message routers if your recipient is not directly accessible to yours. So you may require an address of the format

```
John Rhoton @ A1MBX @ NODE1[JR1] @ NODE2[JR2] @ NODE3[JR3]
@ NODE4[JR4]
```

but if you were already on node four you would require only

```
John Rhoton @ A1MBX @ NODE1[JR5] @ NODE2[JR6] @ NODE3[JR7]
```

and if you were on node one you could get away with

```
John Rhoton @ A1MBX
```

so the address was not universal.

With X.400, my address will always be the same,

```
C=AT;A=ADA;P=Digital;O=Digital;OU=AUI;CN=John Rhoton; or
C=IE;A=EirMail400;P=Digital;S=Rhoton;G=John
```

regardless of where a message originates.

X.400 O/R Addressing

X.400 implements an originator/recipient (O/R) addressing scheme. What this means is that the addresses can be either originators or recipients of a mail message. What this implies, although it is not discernible from the name, is that the addresses are universally applicable and do not stipulate the path of the message.

Let's take a closer look at my X.400 address.

```
C=AT;A=ADA;P=Digital;O=Digital;OU=AUI;CN=John Rhoton; or
C=IE;A=EirMail400;P=Digital;S=Rhoton;G=John
```

It is composed of several fields separated by semicolons. Each has a field name and a field value separated by an "equals" sign. Together they make my address unambiguously refer to my account.

Although the order of the fields is not significant, they are typically ordered in a logical sequence reflecting the hierarchical structure of the addressing scheme. At the top level there is the country, C. ISO has defined a set of two-character country codes, and Austria was assigned the value "AT." Other codes are, for example, "US" for the United States, "IE" for Ireland and "MY" for Malaysia.

Next we have A, the (public) administrative domain (ADMD). Typically, every country will have one or more companies that offer X.400 access to the public and are themselves connected to other countries and administrative domains. Your company will select one of these companies, and its ADMD designation will become yours. In Austria the biggest administrative domain is Radio Austria, designated as "ADA."

There is also a field P, for a private administrative domain (PRMD). While it may be useful to connect several independent companies together to form such a domain, it is more common for each company to have its own private domain. So above you see my employer, "Digital," as my private domain.

The O is the organization, or company, name. It will typically be synonymous with the PRMD above. Often that is enough to enable efficient and unambiguous addressing. You do have the possibility of specifying more than one organizational unit under the OU fields if you wish to map the organizational structure of your company; be careful if you do this, though. It is easy to get carried away and overspecify the addresses. This creates an additional administrative burden when it comes to responding to organizational changes. And it can be very frustrating to external correspondents to have to understand your organizational structure in order to communicate with you. If you have a very large company, like Digital, you may need to introduce some segmentation if for no other reason than to reduce ambiguity when several people have the same name. Be careful to choose organizational units that are short, logical and do not change often. The organizational unit of "AUI" refers to Digital's Austrian headquarters.

Finally, you will need to indicate who your recipient is. The most frequent way of specifying this is with the common name (CN), which is both the given name (G) and the surname (S).

SMTP Addressing

An internet address is typically of the form `Rhoton@mcpserver.msa.dec.com`, where Rhoton is an account name and `mcpserver.msa.dec.com` is the host name of the machine where the account resides. Therefore, we can say that SMTP supports O/R addressing. But we can also specify an explicit path, such as

```
Rhoton@mcpserver.msa.dec.com@mail1.dec.com@mail2.dec.com@mail3.dec.com
```

In this case, the message will be sent first to `mail3.dec.com`, which will relay it to `mail2.dec.com`. There it is again relayed to `mail1.dec.com` and on to `mcpserver.msa.dec.com`, where it is delivered to the appropriate mailbox.

So we actually have both approaches at our disposal. However, I should point out that the second is rarely used since, as we shall see later, DNS takes care of finding an optimal path. Adding additional routing doesn't usually offer any advantage.

X.400 Message Transport System

In keeping with the OSI tradition, X.400 has a splendid architecture. Ease and clarity of implementation may not have been high on the agenda, but there are some clear definitions of what does what in a mailing system. And these can be useful for discussion of any mail model, not only X.400.

User Agent

To use mail, you call up your mail application, browse through all the messages that have arrived for you, and maybe compose some of your own. X.400 calls the piece of software you are using the user agent (UA), since it interacts with the mail backbone on behalf of the user.

X.400 is not concerned with additional functions offered by your application. Microsoft Outlook, for example, provides calendars, contact management and task management functions, as well as supporting many customer-written applications. Most mail programs also support a file cabinet (also known as "personal folders" or "drawers") of sorts, where users can organize their messages and other documents.

But X.400 only defines what interfaces the user agent has in order to be able to submit and retrieve mail on behalf of the user.

X.400 is similarly ambivalent when it comes to the implementation of the user agent. The user could be sitting at a character-cell terminal and running a VT application like ALL-IN-1. On the other hand, a PC user might have a client-server UA, such as Microsoft Outlook, accessing Microsoft Exchange. Or you could have a user running an X.400 user agent directly on the PC. All of these constitute user agents. How many tiers they have and which platforms they use is of no consequence.

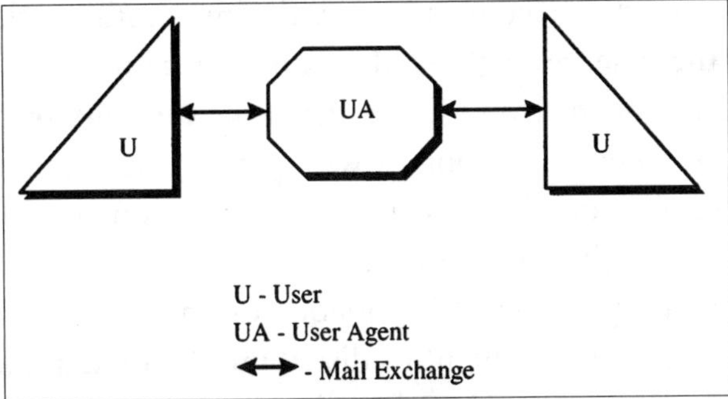

Figure 4-1. *User and User Agent*

The simplest mail configuration you can have is illustrated in Figure 4-1. There is only one user agent, and all the users connect to it. They can send mail to and receive mail from each other but no one else. The user agent handles this local delivery. If this is the configuration, X.400 compliancy of the UA is possible but irrelevant, since it isn't connected anywhere.

Message Transfer Agent

The situation changes when we have a second user agent, as you can see in Figure 4-2. If someone associated with one user agent needs to communicate with another connected to a different UA, we have to establish a connection between the two. It is conceivable that the UAs could find a way to talk to each other directly, but that would require

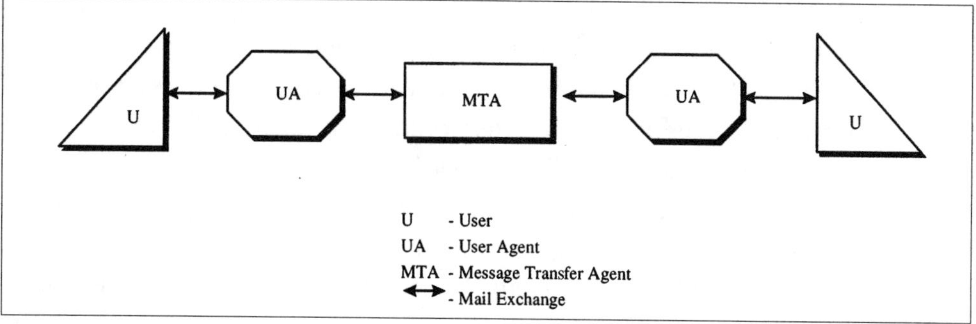

Figure 4-2. *Message Transfer Agent*

the UAs to have direct connections with one another, which is frequently not the case. So we introduce another component called the message transfer agent (MTA). It accepts the message from the UA, takes a look at where it is going (it will typically have more than two attached UAs, so not all messages are going from one UA to the other), and delivers it to the other UA.

As we see in Figure 4-3, it is possible for an organization to have multiple MTAs. You may want to distribute the load among several systems or need to ensure that there is no single point of failure. It could also be that you have several geographically distributed locations and would like to have a local MTA for each place.

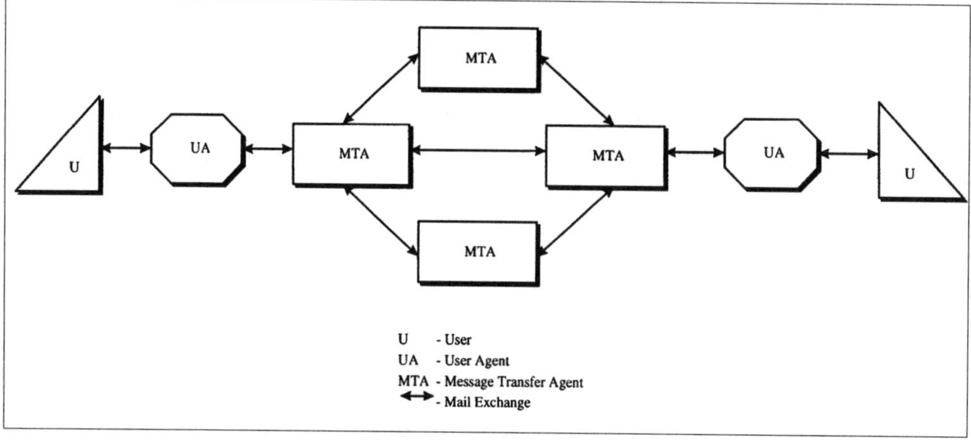

Figure 4-3. *Multiple Message Transfer Agents*

When several MTAs are connected together, they provide functionality called "store-and-forward." What this means is that they do not simply provide a synchronous connection from one user agent to another through all the intermediary MTAs. This would no doubt provide a quicker delivery, but it would not work if any of the links were temporarily disconnected. If you had a long path with a high number of unreliable links, it could be very difficult to get a connection with all of them working at the same time. You might even have restrictions on some of the connections for certain times of the day, which would limit your users as to when they could send mail.

Instead, with multiple MTAs, each MTA receives each message from either a user agent or a peer MTA and stores it locally. When it has finished receiving the mail, it forwards it on to the next step. If the connection is not available, it saves all the messages to that destination in a queue and waits for the connection to be available again. Then it proceeds by sending all the messages on their way.

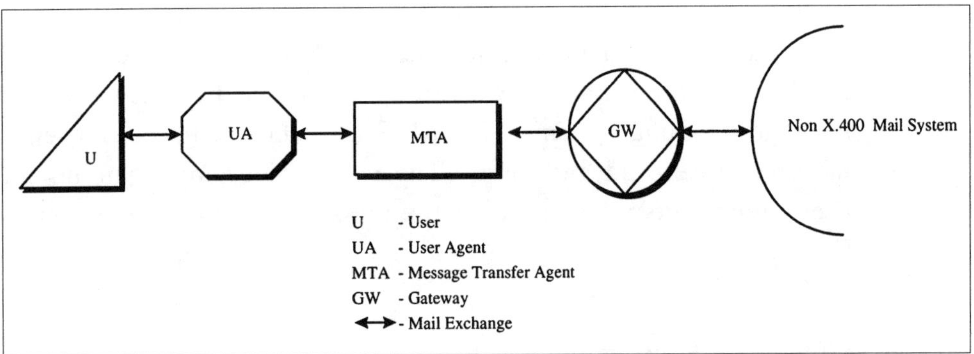

Figure 4-4. *Message Transport System with a Gateway*

The third component, shown in Figure 4-4, is a gateway (GW) or access unit (AU), which provides an interface to another type of messaging system (e.g., Internet or Message Router). This interface makes it possible for users within an X.400 system to communicate with others who use a different mail backbone. It is directly connected to both networks and performs the necessary conversions between them.

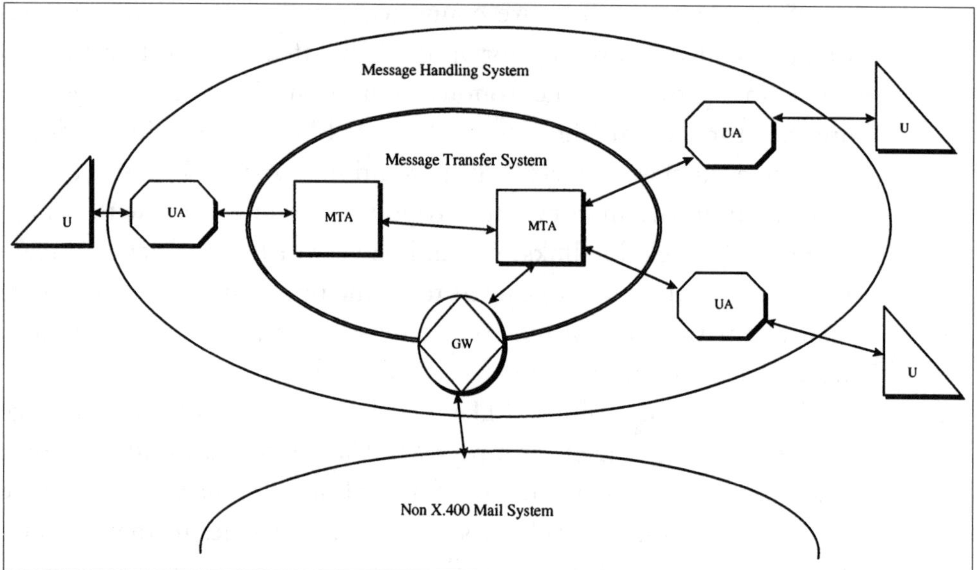

Figure 4-5. *Message Handling Environment*

Figure 4-5 shows the concepts of a message transfer system (MTS) and a message handling system (MHS). The MTS consists of all the MTAs. Several MTSes can be connected by gateways. The message handling system is the MTS plus the agents (user agents, message stores and gateways). The whole diagram, including the users, represents what is called the message handling environment (MHE).

Message Transfer System

In its simplest form, an MTS is a set of directly interconnected MTAs with attached user agents. You can see the familiar example in Figure 4-6. The MTAs can share the same routing information. Each knows of the existence and characteristics of the others. When necessary, they connect to each other to pass messages back and forth.

In Figure 4-7 you can see a more complex topology. It might be that the MTS is not under the jurisdiction of one company, or that it is too large and complex to be centrally managed. In this case, you can

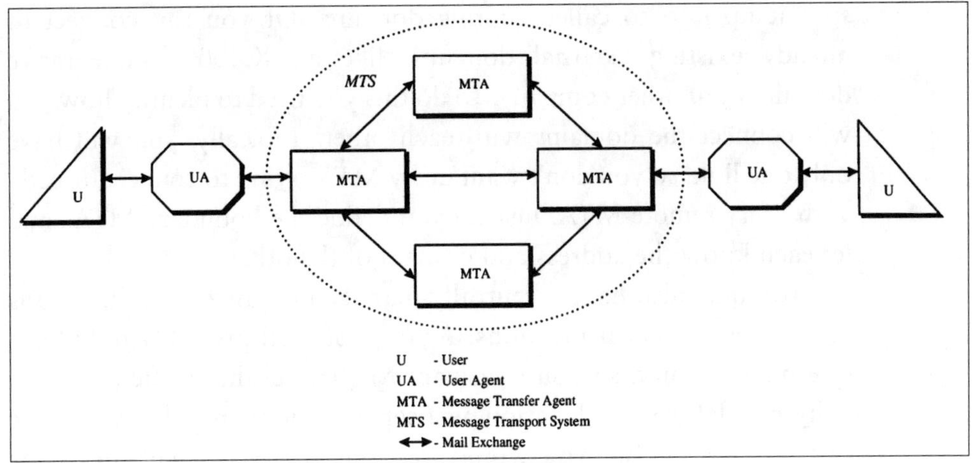

Figure 4-6. *Simple MTS with Single Routing Domain*

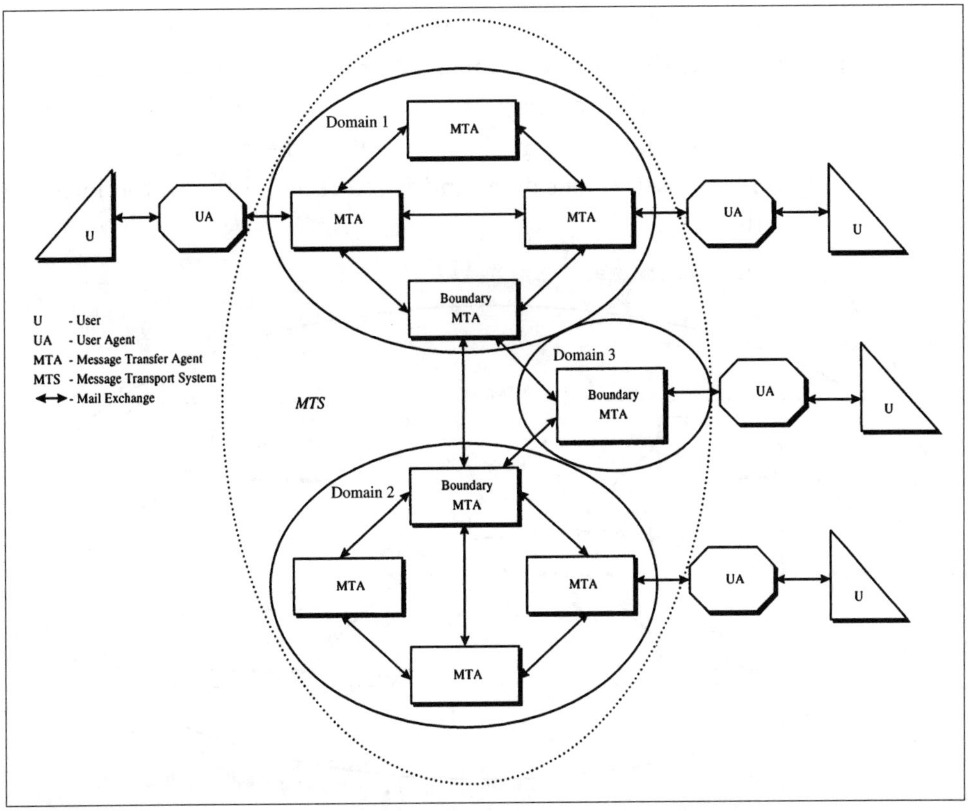

Figure 4-7. *MTS with Multiple Routing Domains*

split it up into so called routing domains. Or you can connect to already existing external domains, like an X.400 administrative domain, or another company. To do this you need to identify how you will connect the domains with each other. Typically, you will have only one link, so you don't want every MTA trying to connect directly with every remote MTA. Instead you define the boundary MTAs and let each know the address and domain of the other.

You may also have a centrally managed organization that spans several geographical locations. Again, you will probably only have one physical link, so you will want to channel the traffic across it. Why not define each location as a separate domain? That would be one alternative. But you would lose the ability to share the same routing data, and consequently make the central management more awkward.

Figure 4-8 shows how you can get what you want with area routing. Arcas are similar to domains, with the significant difference being that they share the routing information within a domain. The area equivalent of the boundary MTA is called the area server. There is only one area server per area, and it redirects all the traffic into and out of the area.

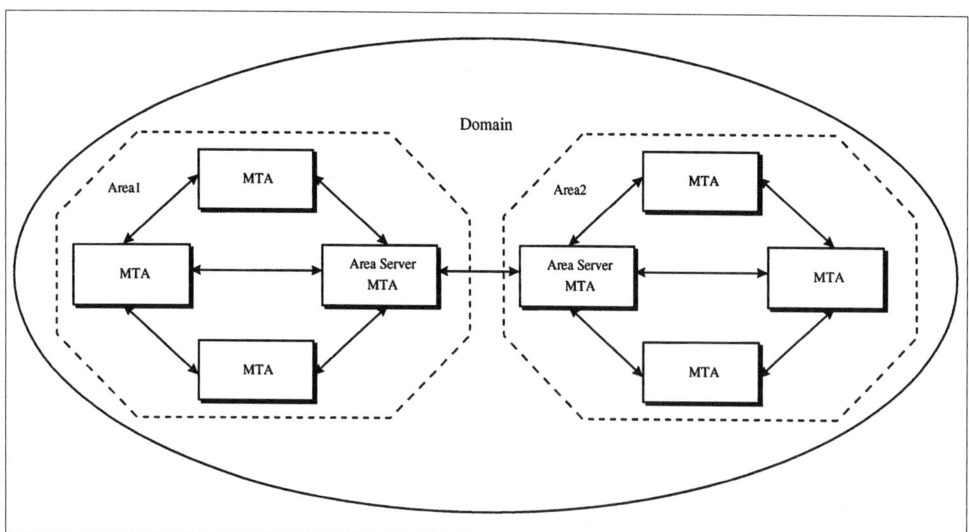

Figure 4-8. *Area Routing*

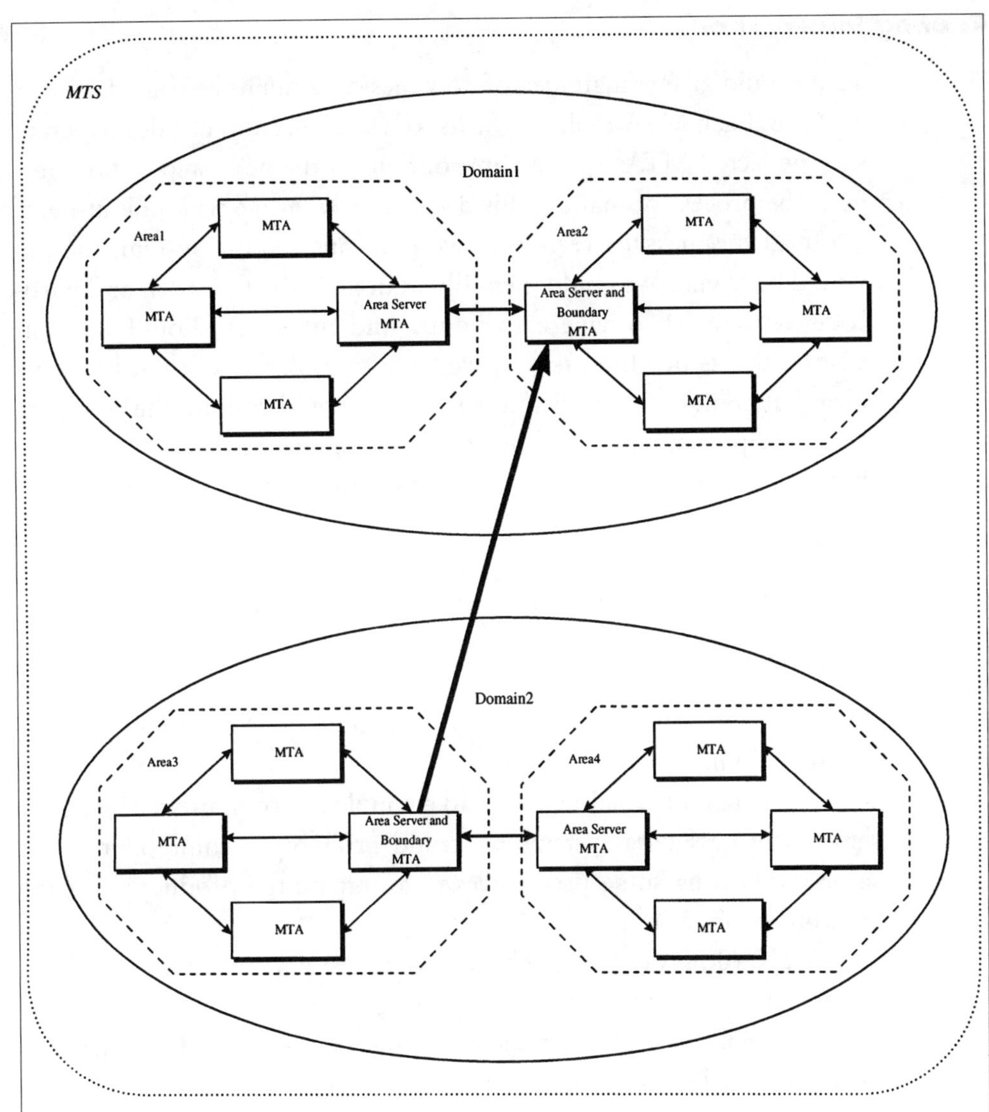

Figure 4-9. *Areas and Domains*

In Figure 4-9 you can see how areas and domains are related. It is not overly complex if you understand both of the concepts. The only thing to keep in mind is that areas are *contained* in domains and are thus subordinate to them.

Routing Information

That should give you an idea of how messages might be routed around an MTS. Each MTA looks at the list of recipients and decides which of the connected MTAs is most appropriate as the next step in the journey. The process of making this decision is what we will look at next.

If all the message recipients were on one remote system, the job would be trivial. We could mentally figure out the best path and hard-code at each MTA where the outbound messages should be sent. Clearly this is not the case, so we have to look for alternatives. One idea that comes to mind is that each MTA could contain the complete list of recipients, with an indication of which peer MTA or user agent lies next in line. To illustrate, we can say that for the recipient

```
C=AT; A=ADA; P=Digital; O=Digital; OU=AUI; CN=John Rhoton
```

we can deliver to the local user agent ALL-IN-1. But for

```
C=US; A=XYZ; P=WhiteHouse; O=WhiteHouse; CN=Bill Clinton
```

we need to transfer the message to the boundary MTA for our administrative domain.

This might be feasible if we had a couple of dozen users. If we only have two messaging systems we could probably accommodate a lot more by writing some procedures to automate the production of the routing information.

But X.400 is designed to be an open messaging environment. This means that we should be able to plug in other domains and user agents at will. Remote user agents should be able to add recipients at any time, and they should be addressable from any user in the messaging environment. If we were connected to the entire world, these exhaustive routing instructions would not be realistic. We would have too many entries.

This is where the hierarchical addressing scheme of X.400 comes to the rescue. We can have routing entries for all of our local users, but there is no need to enter routing information for all of the remote recipients. If, for example, we take the partial address

```
C=US;
```

we can stipulate that all of the messages with this component be routed on to our administrative domain. This is one entry that will take care of the illustrious president and 250 million other Americans in one go. By defining the routing for the other relevant countries, administrative domains and private domains we can efficiently offload to our X.400 service provider all of the routing decisions for messages outside of the company.

Within the company we use the same approach. If we put some thought into the assignment of addresses and the creation of messaging accounts, we should be able to reduce the routing to a small number of entries. We can stipulate that all the messages destined to a particular organizational unit are to be sent on to a given domain, MTA or user agent. In theory, this can be a very elegant and pure solution. In actuality, we will probably have to make a few compromises here and there—companies do not tend to organize with computational efficiency in mind. Nonetheless, the result should be manageable and understandable.

SMTP

SMTP does not emphasize architecture and naming to the extent that X.400 does. Those specifying the SMTP protocols were more interested in getting something that would work than in defining generalities. We can even use the same terminology as X.400, and for the most part the topology will be the same. The most important difference is that an X.400 backbone is closed, whereas an SMTP backbone is open. What this means is that any computer running SMTP will generally accept connections from any other computer running SMTP. In X.400 you would need to explicitly define all peer MTAs, whereas in SMTP all other MTAs on the network are potential peer MTAs. If you don't want this, you must establish and implement restrictions.

SMTP is the mailing approach used on the Internet. On the surface, the configuration shown in Figure 4-10 is fairly similar to what we have already seen. There is some difference in terminology, but nothing major. In actuality, it is more common to refer to the actual implementations of the MUAs and MTAs than these abbreviations.

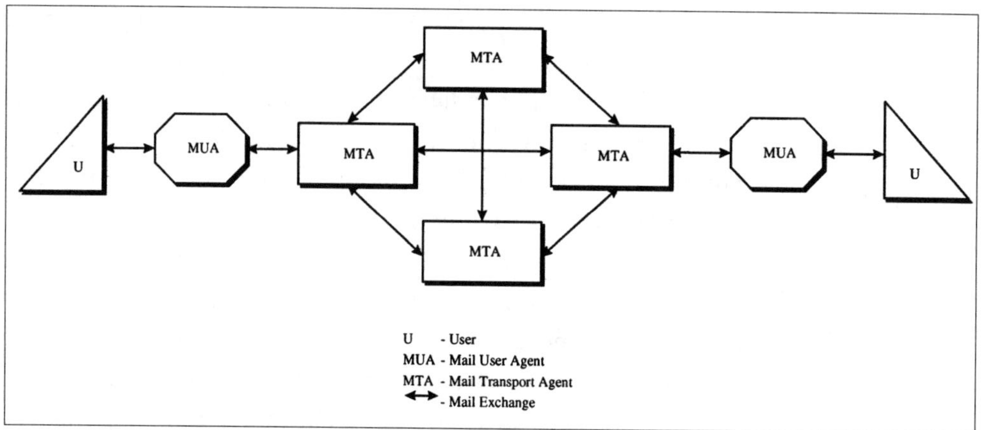

Figure 4-10. *SMTP Network*

On UNIX machines the most common MTA is sendmail. Others include MMDF, Smail 2.x and Zmailer. The standard MUAs on UNIX are Mail or mailx. Other systems don't distinguish so overtly between the MUAs and MTAs. On VMS, PMDF offers an SMTP MTA. And on Windows NT, there is Microsoft Exchange.

Unlike X.400, which runs on an OSI network, SMTP presupposes TCP/IP. And typically, all user nodes in the network are equipped with some support for SMTP. As a result, there is often no difference in the name of the IP host and the name of the MTA. If my username is `rhoton` and my node is `atz02.enet.dec.com` then you can send mail to `rhoton@atz02.enet.dec.com`. And, since all registered nodes on the Internet know each other, you don't really need any routing.

However, there is a way for mail to be addressed other than to the node. We can address to a mail exchange (MX) entry rather than a node name. What this boils down to is that the distributed database (called DNS, for domain name system), which holds all the host records for the entire Internet, also contains these MX records, which resolve to a particular node or set of nodes. Without going into detail, it is significant that the MX records are used to cross firewalls and simplify mail addressing. If you address mail to `John.Rhoton@dbo.mts.dec.com` there is no IP node called `dbo.mts.dec.com` nor account called `John.Rhoton`. Rather, dbo.mts.dec.com represents an MX record indicating one of our firewall computers as the receiving node. From there it is relayed on until it eventually reaches my account.

DNS and SMTP

In addition to performing name-to-address look-ups for systems on the network, DNS provides a mechanism for other applications to store information in a distributed manner. Mail makes use of this to store with a special resource record (RR) called an MX record. The structure of an MX record is: domain name, type (IN), class (MX), preference and host name. An RR of

```
dbo.dec.com     IN     MX     10     mail1.dbo.dec.com
```

would mean that it is possible for mail designated to dbo.dec.com (for example a message to John.Rhoton@dbo.dec.com) to be delivered to the host mail1.dbo.dec.com.

But we can go one step further. If we want to make sure that mail can be delivered even if mail1.dbo.dec.com is down, we can specify multiple resource records for the same domain.

```
dbo.dec.com     IN     MX     10     mail1.dbo.dec.com
dbo.dec.com     IN     MX     10     mail2.dbo.dec.com
dbo.dec.com     IN     MX     20     mail3.dbo.dec.com
dbo.dec.com     IN     MX     30     mail4.dbo.dec.com
```

Message Stores

In some cases the user agent is not online or has only periodic connections to the MTA. This poses a problem for the MTA, which is charged with delivering messages to the user agent. To solve this problem, the 1988 standard has accommodated the notion of a message store (MS) that is always connected to the MTA. As shown in Figure 4-11, it sends messages to the MTA and receives them from it. The user agent can connect to the message store whenever it is convenient and exchange messages.

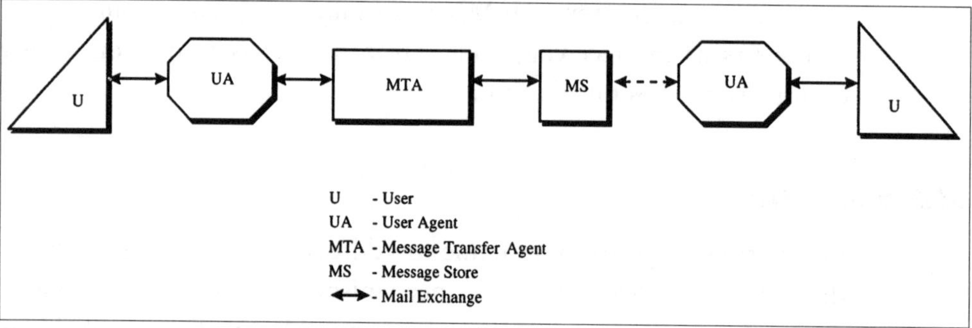

Figure 4-11. *Message Store*

A message store is a lot like a primitive file cabinet. It stores a set of inbound and a set of outbound messages for each user. But unlike any commercially available file cabinet, it doesn't support any more structure than that.

The UA will periodically connect to the MS, retrieve all the messages for a given user or set of users, and possibly request the submission of some others. If the MTA is reachable at that point in time, the submission goes on to the MTA. Otherwise, the messages remain at the MS until it can establish a connection with the MTA.

X.400 Message Store

OSI expanded the X.400 architecture to accommodate a message store in 1988. In doing so, it also added a protocol (P7) for communication between the user agent and the message store.

POP3

Post office protocol—version 3 (POP3) is described in RFC 1939. As you can guess from the name, it had a number of predecessors. POP was defined in 1984, followed by POP2, and in 1988 the first version of POP3 was defined. It has been refined a few times since and has established itself as a widespread standard.

A POP3 server is really a lot like a message store in the X.400 world. It enables mail delivery to PCs that are not always connected to the network. The server accepts SMTP mail from the network and stores it for later retrieval by the client.

The client can connect to the server using the POP3 protocol and download all of the mail into a local store, where the user can read and respond to it. After the client retrieves the mail, it is typically deleted on the server, so the user does all further processing on the local client.

Note that POP3 is a retrieval-only protocol. To send mail, the client uses a normal SMTP connection to the destination (or at least the nearest mail server). The only purpose of the protocol is to support occasional disconnection; when the client needs to send mail, it can always make a connection.

Understanding the POP3 protocol is not particularly difficult. A client first needs to establish a TCP connection to the POP3 server, usually at port 110. It then enters what is called the authorization state. At this point the client must provide a username and password.

Once the user has been authenticated, the connection enters the transaction state. The client can then ask for mailbox listings and retrieve and delete messages from the mailbox. The keywords for the minimal POP3 commands are listed in Table 4-1; Appendix D shows a sample POP3 transaction.

Table 4-1. *POP3 Commands*

Keyword	Description
USER	Supply username for mailbox
PASS	Supply password for mailbox
STAT	Request the number of messages and total size of message
LIST	List the index and size of all messages
RETR	Retrieve the specified messages
DELE	Delete the specified message
NOOP	No action required
RSET	Rollback message deletion
QUIT	Update (commit) message deletion and terminate connection

IMAP4

POP3 has a distinct disadvantage for a number of users. Users who move around a lot (also called roaming users) often need to use different PCs. With POP3, their mail it is gone once they have retrieved it from the server. This means that if the user switches to a different PC the old mail will be inaccessible. What is needed is a protocol that will allow the user the option of downloading the mail to the PC (where the access will be quicker and fewer server resources are needed) or of leaving the mail on the server and allowing remote online access to the messages. This is where the Internet message access protocol—version 4 (IMAP4) comes in. IMAP4 significantly extends the functionality of the POP3 protocol to allow both offline and online storage of the messages. It also provides a number of other functions:

- Allows user-initiated storage of objects;
- Allows storage of non-mail objects;
- Has facilities for user configuration management;
- Allows sharing of mailboxes.

In fact, it is very much a full-fledged file cabinet.

The commands of IMAP4, shown in Table 4-2, are not unlike those of POP3, but there are many more of them. For a full description of the functions you can refer to RFC 2060.[1]

Since POP3 has been around a lot longer, there is much more software available to support it than IMAP4. The situation is expected to change, however. IMAP4 offers more functionality than POP3 and has no real disadvantage. As a result, the market has embraced IMAP4 as the protocol of the future.

---

[1] RFC 2060 specifies IMAP4rev1; i.e., the first revision of IMAP4. IMAP is still being refined and extended, so this may not be the final version. If you want more information on IMAP, you might also want to take a look at http://www.imap.org/

Table 4-2. *IMAP4 Commands*

Command	Description
CAPABILITY	Request listing of functionality of server
AUTHENTICATE	Indicates an authentication mechanism
LOGIN	Identifies client with username and password
SELECT	Selects the mailbox to use
EXAMINE	Select mailbox in read-only mode
CREATE	Create a mailbox
DELETE	Delete a mailbox
RENAME	Rename a mailbox
SUBSCRIBE	Add mailbox to server's set of active mailboxes
UNSUBSCRIBE	Remove mailbox from server's set of active mailboxes
LIST	List set or subset of mailboxes
LSUB	List subscribed mailboxes
STATUS	Requests the status (e.g. total number, unseen number of messages) of mailbox
APPEND	Add a message to the mailbox
CHECK	Request checkpoint of mailbox
CLOSE	Effects pending deletions and closes mailbox
EXPUNGE	Effects pending deletions
SEARCH	Searches mailbox for messages satisfying given criteria
FETCH	Fetches specified bodyparts for a given message
STORE	Changes data of specified messages in the mailbox
COPY	Copies a message to another mailbox
NOOP	No action required
LOGOUT	Close the connection

Highlights

- X.400 and SMTP both use essentially the same component to perform message transfer.
- X.400 defines a clear architecture. SMTP puts less focus on definitions and more on function.
- Both X.400 and SMTP offer destination addressing. SMTP also offers explicit routing, but this is seldom used.
- Neither address is particularly attractive, but many prefer the SMTP address, which tends to be shorter and is potentially more mnemonic.

- X.400 offers a closed backbone where all peer MTAs must be declared to each other. SMTP uses an open backbone where any MTA can talk to any other MTA.
- Both approaches offer facilities for discontinuous connections:
    - X.400 offers the P7 protocol.
    - Internet offers POP3 and IMAP4; MAP4 will probably replace POP3.

References

Albitz, Paul, and C. Liu. 1992. *DNS and BIND*. Sebastopol, CA: O'Reilly and Associates, Inc. ISBN 1-56592-010-4.

Black, Ulysses. 1995. *TCP/IP and Related Protocols*. New York: McGraw-Hill. ISBN 0-07-113296-1.

Costales, Bryan. 1993. *Sendmail*. Sebastopol, CA: O'Reilly and Associates, Inc. ISBN 1-56592-056-2.

Crispin, M. 1996. *Internet Message Access Protocol—Version 4rev1* (RFC 2060).

Hunt, Craig. 1992. *TCP/IP Network Administration*. Sebastopol, CA: O'Reilly and Associates, Inc. ISBN 1-937175-82-X.

Mockapetris, P. 1983. *Domain Names—Concepts and Facilities* (RFC 882).

Mockapetris, P. 1983. *Domain Names—Implementation and Specification* (RFC 883).

Myers, J., and M. Rose. 1996. *Post Office Protocol—Version 3* (RFC 1939).

Partridge, C. 1986. *Mail Routing and the Domain System* (RFC 974).

Postel, J. 1982. *Simple Mail Transfer Protocol* (RFC 821).

Radicati, S. 1992. *Electronic Mail: An Introduction to the X.400 Message Handling Standards*. New York: McGraw-Hill. ISBN 0-07-051104-7.

Chapter 5

Message Transfer

We now know what a message looks like and what path it traverses to get from its source to its destination. What is missing is a closer look at how a message is transferred from one system to the next.

In this area there are a few points to focus on:

1. We need to establish the protocols of mail transfer.
2. In the case of store-and-forward (both X.400 and SMTP), we need an interim storage.
3. We need to decide at each system where the next step toward the destination is.

X.400 Protocols

Figure 5-1 shows the protocols defined by the ITU–T for communication between the messaging components. P1 defines the protocol to be used between two adjacent MTAs. If an MTA does not support P1, it cannot be said to conform to X.400 and it cannot interoperate with other X.400-compliant MTAs. P2 is similarly important, as it defines what a user agent can expect from another user agent. As we saw earlier, this is called the content of a message, and

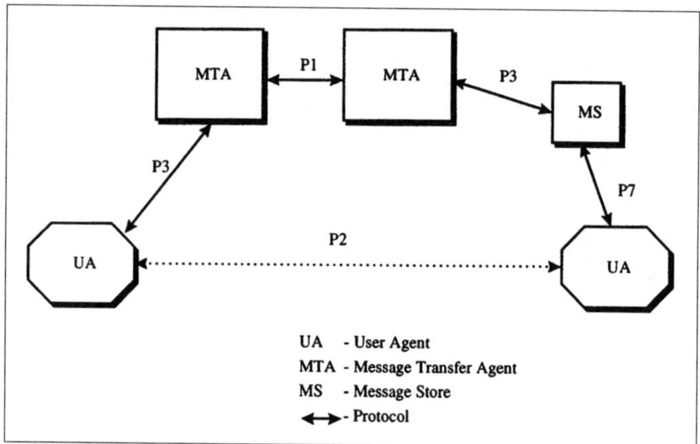

Figure 5-1. *X.400 Protocols*

it should conform to a certain structure or the recipient UA will not be able to use it.

The relationship between P1 and P2 is quite similar to the relationship between the protocols at different layers in the OSI stack. P2 describes the content of a message. P1 will include messages in its protocol, so it essentially packages the P2 protocol with some control information (the envelope).

When a message store is in use, the user agent will need to communicate with it using P7. This protocol defines how to submit and receive messages from the store.

P3 is the protocol used by both message store and user agent to communicate with the MTA. Note that it is not customarily implemented. Instead, the application programming interface called XAPI, defined by X/Open and XAPIA (X.400 Application Programming Interface Association) is used. The interface specifications are available from X/Open.

X.400 Message Transfer Agents

The message transfer agent is the workhorse of an X.400 network. The MTA takes care of moving messages around the network and performs all necessary conversions to make the documents available to the intended recipients. We will examine in more detail the routing and conversion in the next section, but first let us take a brief look at the structure of an MTA.

Message Flow

In Figure 5-2 you can see the logical picture of how an X.400 MTA structures its components. The main component is in the center and is called the message processor. It analyses every MPDU and decides what to do with it. By looking at the envelope and comparing the recipients' addresses to the routing instructions it has in its database, it is able to determine whether the messages should be locally delivered or forwarded on to another MTA. Accordingly, it places the MPDU in either the delivery queue or the relay queue, where the corresponding entities can retrieve it at their leisure. The message processor also performs a number of other operations, such as splitting the MPDUs for recipients at multiple destinations, converting bodyparts, resolving redirection and distribution lists and monitoring the routing cycle for loops.

On the left-hand side we have the agents. These can be user agents, message stores or gateways. They can connect to the MTA and, via the interface region, pull any message destined to them out of the delivery

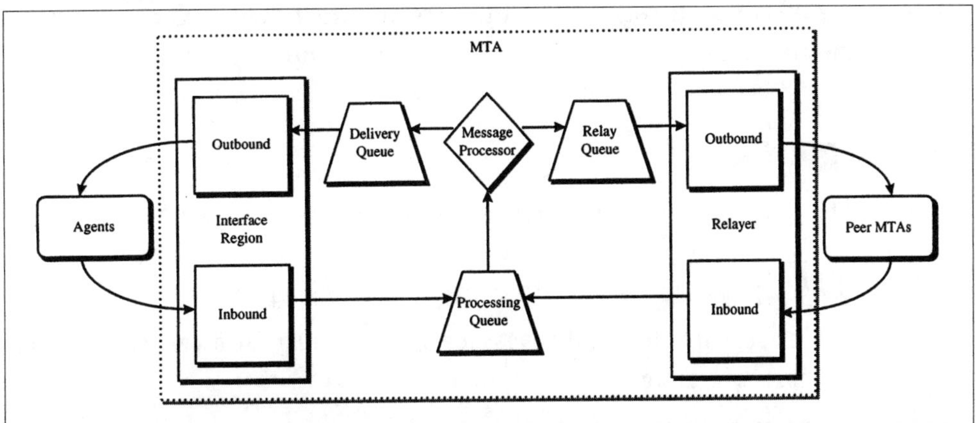

Figure 5-2. *MTA Queues and Processors*

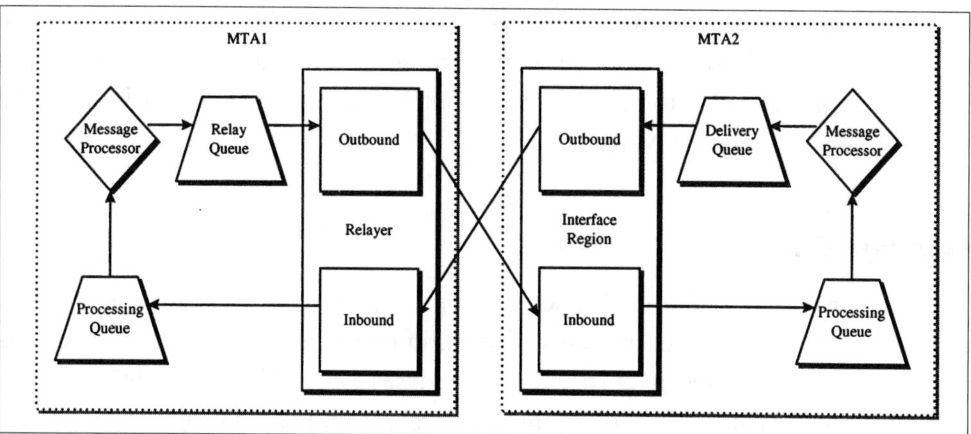

Figure 5-3. *Peer MTA Communication*

queue. Often they will also submit messages to the MTA. In this case the messages are placed in the processing queue, where the message processor can retrieve them to route them to their destinations.

The relayer is analogous to the interface region. Peer MTAs, as shown in Figure 5-3, are able to connect to an MTA and retrieve all of their messages out of the relay queue. On the other side, these MPDUs are placed in the processing queue to be analyzed by the peer's message processor. This process is, of course, bi-directional, so the peer may also have outgoing messages to our MTA, which we would then need to forward. Let's see whether we can put all of the X.400 concepts together and understand how they each contribute to the routing of a message from one user to another.

Message Routing

There are four steps to the routing of a message by the MTS:

1. Accepting the message from an (originator) agent
2. Temporarily storing the message while waiting for a connection to the next MTA or agent
3. Routing the message to the next MTA
4. Delivering the message to the (recipient) agent

Steps 1 and 4 occur only once in the life-cycle of an MPDU, but steps 2 and 3 may occur any number of times.

Let's take a look at the routing as it is represented in Figure 5-4. The user U1 connects to his user agent UA1, and submits a message

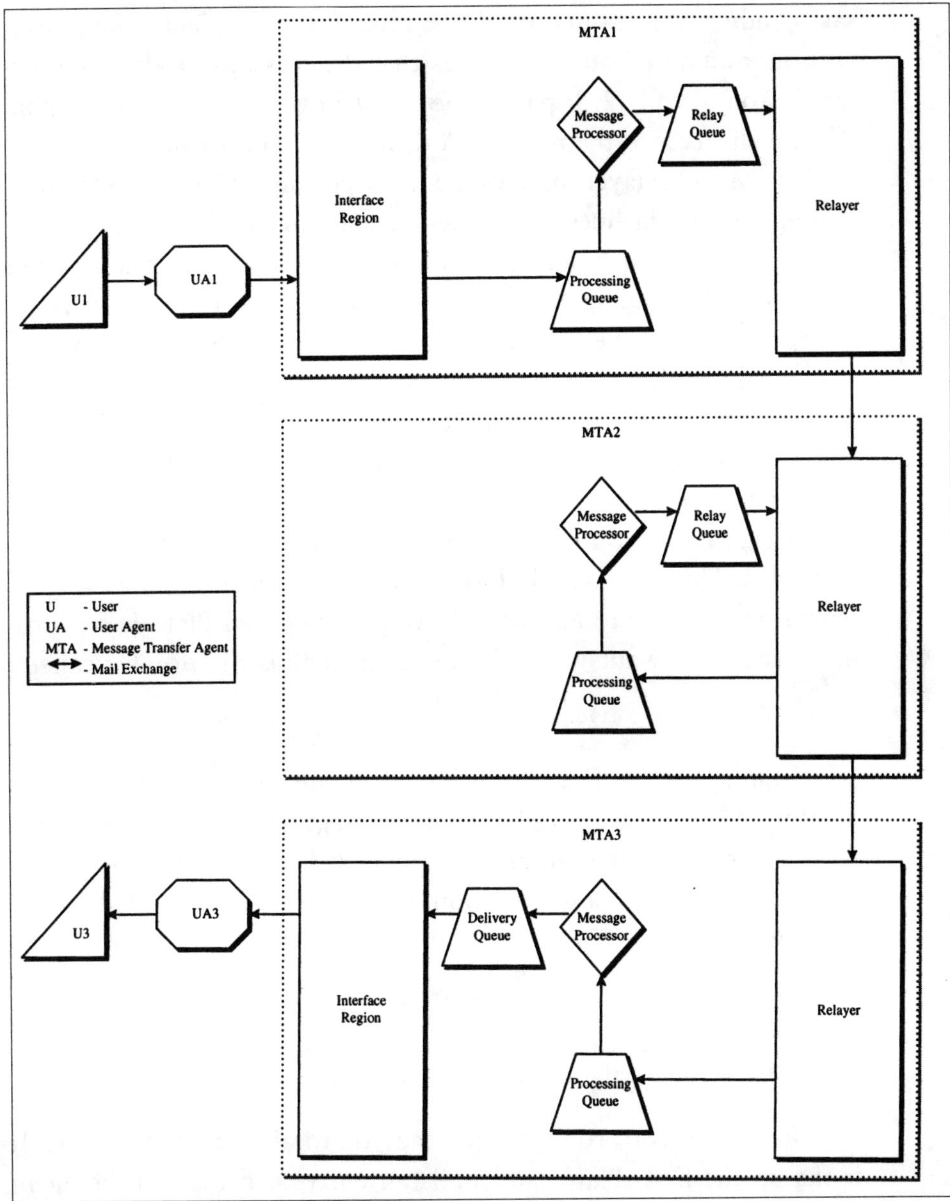

Figure 5-4. *Message Flow Through the MTAs*

for user U3. The user agent creates an ASN.1 object for the message using the XOM interface and then submits the message via the XAPI interface to its MTA, MTA1. There it is received in the interface region and is placed in the processing queue for the message processor to attend to. Eventually the MP wades through its backlog of messages and arrives at ours. It takes a look at the recipient, compares it with its routing database and sees that the message needs to be forwarded on to MTA2. It passes the MPDU on to the interface region, which delivers it to the peer MTA using the P1 protocol.

The MTA2 relayer receives the message and places it into the processing queue. This message processor does much the same as its predecessor except that it identifies MTA3 as the next step. The message is relayed there and again goes into the processing queue at MTA3.

When MTA3's message processor looks at the routing information, it sees that the MPDU should be locally delivered to the user agent UA3. It looks up how to invoke it and then passes it the message via the XAPI interface. UA3 gratefully receives the message and decodes it with the XOM interface. It then stores the message for retrieval by the user.

In Figure 5-5 you can see a familiar picture of routing domains and areas. This time we will look at what happens when a message is sent from one user to another. We will assume that Plato is our prolific writer who wants to send a message to a distribution list called

```
C=GR; A=XCD; O=Philosophers; CN=Greek-Philosophers.
```

He uses his favorite user agent to create the message, which is transmitted to `Area1.MTA12`. There the message processor examines the message and finds the DL as a recipient. It looks up its routing data and finds that this is a distribution list and must be expanded, which it promptly does:

```
C=GR; A=XCD; O=Philosophers; OU=A1; CN=Plato
C=GR; A=XCD; O=Philosophers; OU=A2; CN=Aristoteles
C=GR; A=XCD; O=Philosophers; OU=A3; CN=Socrates
C=GR; A=XCD; O=Philosophers; OU=A4; CN=Pythagoras
```

Now it needs to route the message on to all four destinations. It looks up the first (Plato) and finds an entry to deliver to the agent Plato-UA on this MTA, so it passes the MPDU on to the user agent.

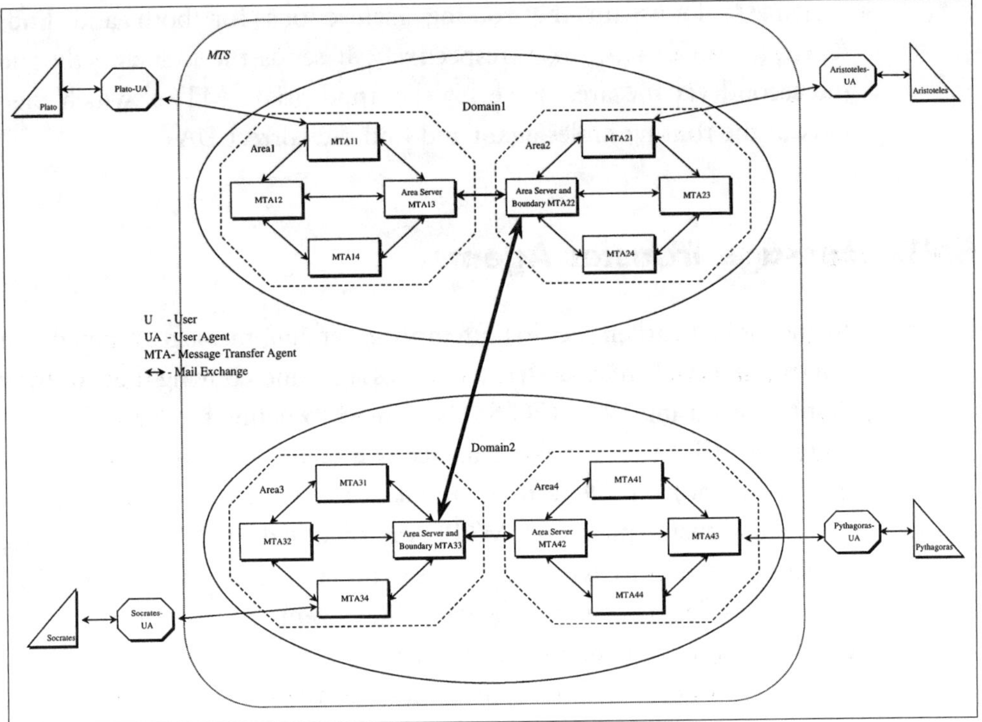

Figure 5-5. *Message Routing Across Domains*

But there are other destinations as well, so it needs to split (make a copy of) the MPDU for the rest.

It looks up the second address (Aristoteles) and sees that it needs to be delivered to the agent Aristoteles-UA on the MTA `Area2.MTA23`. It also looks at the third and fourth entries and finds that it needs to transfer their messages to the domain `Domain2`.

But `Area2.MTA23` is a different area and `Area1.MTA12` is not the area server. And the boundary MTA for `Domain2` is not in this area either. So it figures out the area server (`Area1.MTA13`) and passes the MPDU off to it. Now we are at the area server, so we can establish a direct connection to `Area2.MTA12` and relay the message again. Finally we are in the right area and can send the message directly to the MTA responsible for Aristoteles, which delivers it to his UA.

At the same time we are also at the boundary MTA, so we can connect to `Area3.MTA13` and deliver both Socrates' and Pythagoras' messages.

`Area3.MTA13` looks up the routing instructions for both and finds `Area3.MTA34` and `Area4.MTA43`, respectively. It sends the first directly and the second via the area server to the appropriate MTAs, which then look at the routing tables again and find the correct UAs.

SMTP Message Transfer Agents

As mentioned earlier, the first attempts at sending messages through the Internet involved creating structured messages and copying them to their destinations using FTP. RFC 561 was used to define the structure, and eventually FTP was extended to accommodate messages. But mail is quite different from file transfer, and it clearly needed its own standard.

Mail transfer protocol (MTP) was specified in RFC 772 leaning heavily on its predecessor, FTP. This protocol was refined in RFC 780 and reclassified as "simple" in RFC 788. Eventually, the current standard for SMTP was defined in RFC 821.

SMTP involves relaying messages from one MTA to another in adherence to the SMTP protocol defined in the RFC. It specifies that a sending MTA must initiate a TCP connection with the intended recipient's MTA, using port 25.

Table 5-1. *SMTP Commands*

Command	Description
HELO	Identify sender
MAIL	Initiate mail transfer with indication of originator
RCPT	Identify one of the recipients
DATA	Indicate readiness to send text of message
RSET	Reset mail transfer
VRFY	Verify mail address
EXPN	Expand distribution list
HELP	Request help on command
NOOP	Do nothing
QUIT	Request termination of connection

The MTA then begins sending a sequence of commands, which you can see listed in Table 5-1. After each command it waits for confirmation from the receiving MTA. This confirmation is in the form of a numeric three-digit status, structured with the first digit indicating the success status and the second the class of response. Possible values for the first digit are:

1. Positive preliminary reply (pending confirmation);
2. Positive completion reply;
3. Positive intermediate reply (requires more information);
4. Transient negative completion reply (temporary error condition);
5. Permanent negative completion reply.

Possible values for the second digit are:

0. Syntax;
1. Information;
2. Connections;
3. Unspecified;
4. Unspecified;
5. Mail system.

The third digit has no particular meaning other than to distinguish between possible valid responses having the same first two digits. The list of standard three-digit responses is included in the RFC.

Now, on to a simple example:

Sender:	`mail from:<John.Rhoton@dbo.mts.dec.com>`
Receiver:	`250 OK – mail from <John.Rhoton@dbo.mts.dec.com>`
Sender:	`rcpt to:<Raj.Ilanko@msa.mts.dec.com>`
Receiver:	`250 OK – Recipient <Raj.Ilanko@msa.mts.dec.com>`
Sender:	`data`
Receiver:	`354 Send data. End with CRLF.CRLF`
Sender:	`This is the first line.`

Sender:	`This is the second line.`
Sender:	`.`
Receiver:	`250 OK`
Sender:	`quit`
Receiver:	`221 closing connection`

Here we see a mail transaction that begins with the sender indicating the mail address of the originator. It can specify any address that adheres to the SMTP address syntax. The recipient MTA will not validate whether the address actually exists or whether the message really comes from the specified originator.

Since the syntax is all right, it sends a success status back. The only important part of the reply line is the "250." The rest is simply informative. Taking apart the status, we first have a "2," which means that it is a positive completion reply. The "5" tells us that it refers to the mail system.

The sending MTA now knows that the first command worked, so it can send the second one. It proceeds by specifying the recipient's mail address. Again, the receiving MTA indicates that it understood the mail command with a "250" response.

Now that the addresses have been established, the sender can deliver the actual message. It does this by sending the command DATA. The receiver understands this command, but it cannot send a positive completion reply because the command is not complete. The sender has only indicated what it intends to do; namely, transfer the message. So the receiver uses a positive intermediate reply with the value of "354."

The sender can now send the message. The text that is sent in this data portion is the actual message. It must adhere to the syntax specified in RFC 822. At the end the sender sends a line containing a single dot. And then the receiver can finally acknowledge the successful completion of the data transfer.

When the sender requests a termination of the connection with QUIT we see a different second digit. This does not apply to the mail system, but rather to the connection itself, which carries a value of 2.

Routing and the Domain System

The previous example assumes that a single connection is possible between the sender and recipient and the message is transferred directly from one MTA to the other. If you are running on the same LAN or even an intra-company WAN (wide area network) with high bandwidth and high availability, then this may be possible. Otherwise we need to have a way of supporting store-and-forward functionality in the message system.

To illustrate this, take a look at Figure 5-6. Let us assume that an Irish user connected to the MTA `dublin.dbo.dec.com` needs to send a message to a Malaysian user on `kuala-lumpur.msa.dec.com`. The `dublin` MTA will look up the MX record for `kuala-lumpur.msa.dec.com` and find four entries. It starts by trying the one with the lowest preference value, which is `kuala-lumpur` itself, with 10.

If the connection is possible then we have a single-hop mail delivery and we are done. But it may be the case that the system is offline or that the line to Asia is down. So `dublin` needs to keep looking. The next entry is `singapore`, with a preference value of 20. The `dublin` machine tries this MTA and is unsuccessful again. So we have a final attempt to `reading` which, in our example, is successful.

Note that if it had not been able to transfer to `dublin`, it would need to store the message in an internal queue and wait until one of

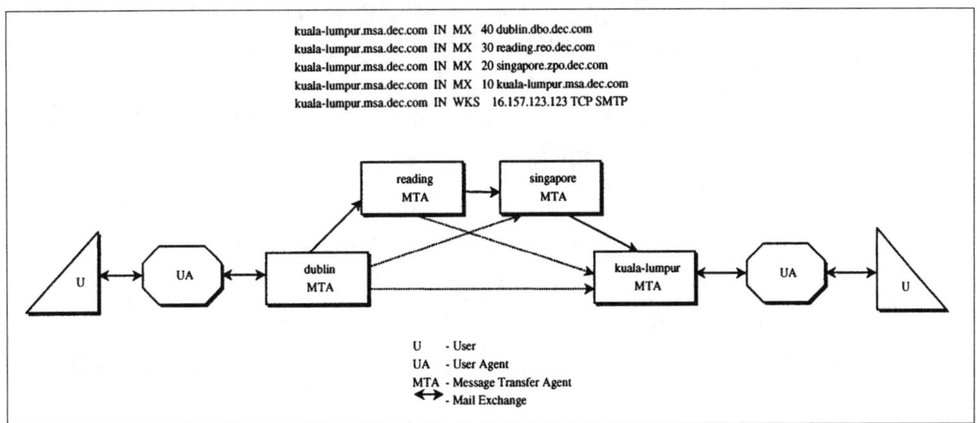

Figure 5-6. *SMTP Routing and DNS*

the connections became possible. There would be no point in trying its own record—it would just be sending mail to itself.

Now `reading` has the message and needs to go through the same sequence. It is successful on the second attempt and passes the message on to `singapore`. But, before we go on, let us look at what would have happened if `singapore` had not been available either. It would have obviously skipped its own record with a preference value of 30 to avoid looping on itself. What is perhaps less obvious is that it would also ignore `dublin`'s record, since it has a higher preference value than its own.

This is one of the features of preferences. A mail system can only relay messages to others with lower MX preferences than its own. If we did not have this restriction, we could have `dublin` and `reading` sending mail back and forth ad infinitum!

Back to the example, the message is now in `singapore` and will remain there until the link between `singapore` and `kuala-lumpur` is available, since there are no other lower preference records available. When our link goes up, the message is delivered to `kuala-lumpur` and the user can read the message.

In this description I mentioned only the MX records. There are, however, other resource records that can come into play in the mail routing. We obviously have the A (host address) records, which tell us what the IP addresses of `kuala-lumpur.msa.dec.com` and the other MTA machines are. The MX records give us only the name of the mail hosts, so we have to look up the records to make the actual IP connection. And then there are the WKS (well-known services) records. It could be that one of the hosts specified in the MX records does not support TCP and SMTP, but rather some other mail protocol. This is highly unlikely, but if we want to be safe we can look up which services the various machines support. Examining the list indicated in their WKS records would do this. To be formally correct we would therefore make the check. However, we would also find out soon enough if we just attempted to make the connection and saw whether it was successful.

Highlights

- Both X.400 and SMTP implement store-and-forward functionality.
- X.400 MTAs communicate via the P1 protocol.
- SMTP MTAs communicate via the SMTP (RFC 821) protocol.
- P1 is terse and succinct.
- SMTP is readable and easy to use and implement, but more verbose.
- X.400 performs routing using routing tables manually configured for the domain.
- SMTP routes by looking up entries in the global DNS.

References

Albitz, Paul, and C. Liu. 1992. *DNS and BIND*. Sebastopol, CA: O'Reilly & Associates, Inc. ISBN 1-56592-010-4.

Black, Ulysses. 1995. *TCP/IP & Related Protocols*. New York: McGraw-Hill. ISBN 0-07-113296-1.

Partridge, C. 1986. *Mail Routing and the Domain System.* (RFC 974).

Postel, J. 1982. *Simple Mail Transfer Protocol* (RFC 821).

Radicati, S. 1992. *Electronic Mail: An Introduction to the X.400 Message Handling Standards.* New York: McGraw-Hill. ISBN 0-07-051104-7.

Chapter 6

Directory Service

Directory Service and Mail

While a directory service is really a topic for its own book, it has historically been quite closely related to discussions of mail. In fact, some mail systems, like MAILbus 400 and Microsoft Exchange, even store their configuration data in the directory tree, so we cannot avoid a short venture into the idea of directories.

The fact that an X.500 directory is distributed across the network makes it an ideal repository for mail configuration data, which must be accessed from many points in the network. Additionally, you may populate the tree with your own information. This usually includes, but is not limited to, entries for all of your users. Some of the mail users agents (like ALL-IN-1 3.2) make this easy for you by automatically adding an entry for every account created and applying subsequent changes of the account to the entry. In other cases you will have to add the users manually or write scripts to enter them.

X.500 Directory Information Tree

In theory, it would be possible to store the data for either in a relational database. This would make the implementation trivial but not the most efficient. As illustrated in Figure 6-1, organizations are

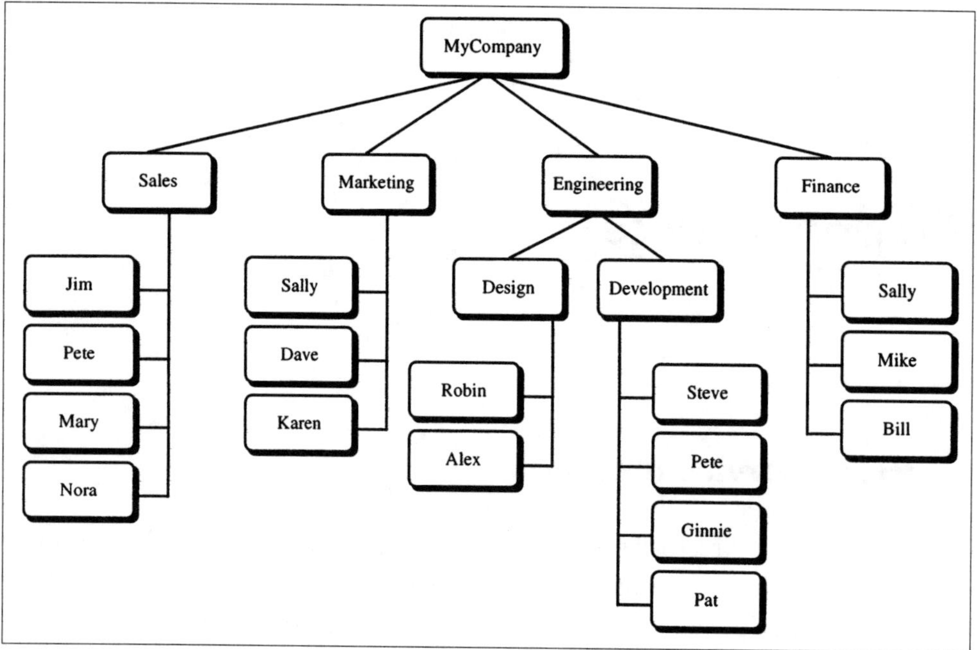

Figure 6-1. *Organizational Structure Tree*

typically hierarchically structured. To optimize access and maintenance of the data, a tree-structured database has been selected to store the directory entries.

If you take a look at Figure 6-2, you will see what X.500 calls a directory information tree (DIT). We have given each entry a name and a value. So you have entries labeled "O=MyCompany," "OU=Finance," or "CN=Sally." These labels help the information tree identify the entries. But they alone are not enough to uniquely specify an address. If you look carefully you will see that there are two entries labeled "CN=Sally." One is under Marketing and the other under Finance. Of course, not all organizations are this informal, with people called exclusively by their first names. When you specify both a given name and a surname to form a common name, there is much less likelihood of a clash. But it still cannot be guaranteed.

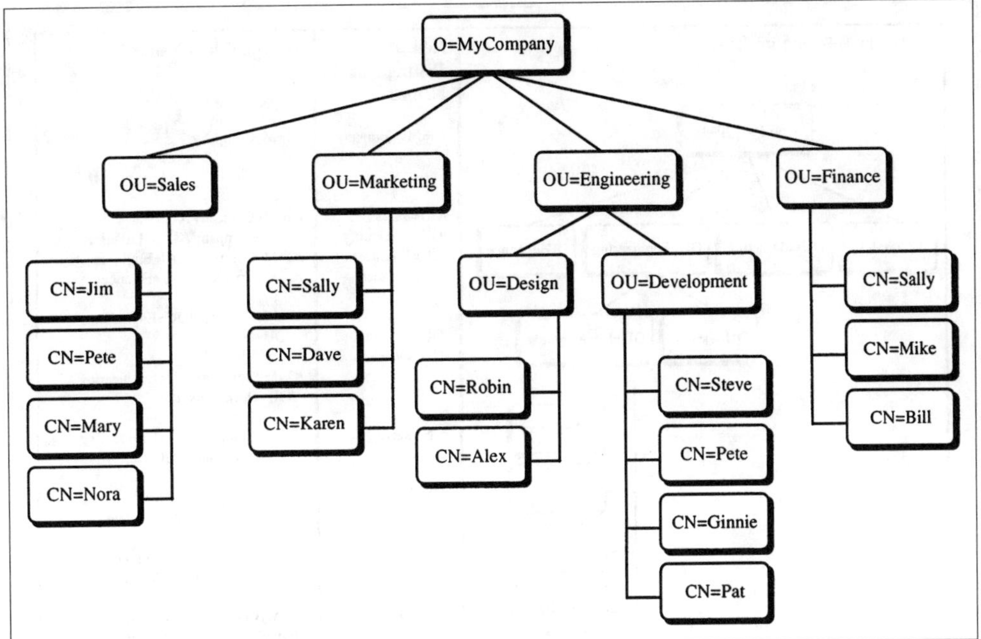

Figure 6-2. *X.500 Tree*

To ensure that we have unique entries, we need to specify the whole path: "O=MyCompany, OU=Finance, CN=Sally" or "O=MyCompany, OU=Marketing, CN=Sally." There are two notations in widespread use to represent these keys. The first is `(O=MyCompany, OU=Marketing, CN=Sally)` and the other is `/O=MyCompany /OU=Marketing /CN=Sally`. Digital X.500 uses the latter, so I will also use it here. Don't let this confuse you, though, if you see the other elsewhere.

The name given to the full key is distinguished name (DN). It fully distinguishes itself from all the other entries (i.e., it is unique). We also have a name, the relative distinguished name (RDN), for the (usually final) part of the distinguished name that serves to uniquely identify itself among its siblings (the children of its parents).

So if we take the example in Figure 6-3 of Pat in Engineering, we can traverse the tree starting at the top. The root is the only entry whose DN matches its RDN (`/O=MyCompany`). The next level is

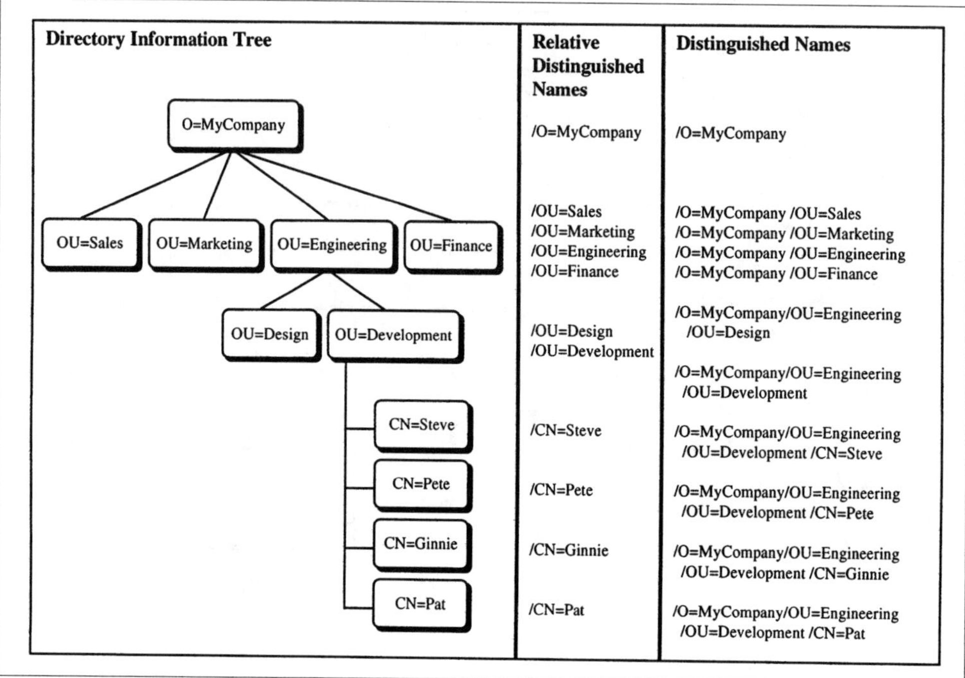

Figure 6-3. *Distinguished Names*

Engineering with a DN of `/O=MyCompany /OU=Engineering` and an RDN of `/OU=Engineering`. The same thing happens with Development, and finally Pat, who has a DN of `CN=Pat` and an RDN of `/O=MyCompany /OU=Engineering /OU=Development /CN=Pat`.

We will be mostly concerned with DNs, since they are what we use to look up entries. So using one of the DNs above, we can look up information on the corporation, its engineering division, its development department, or one of its employees, like Pat.

Directory Services Model

The directory information tree is managed by an entity called the directory system agent (DSA). It manages access to the data and ensures that it is always up to date. But the DSAs are not meant to be invoked by the users directly. Instead, there is another software

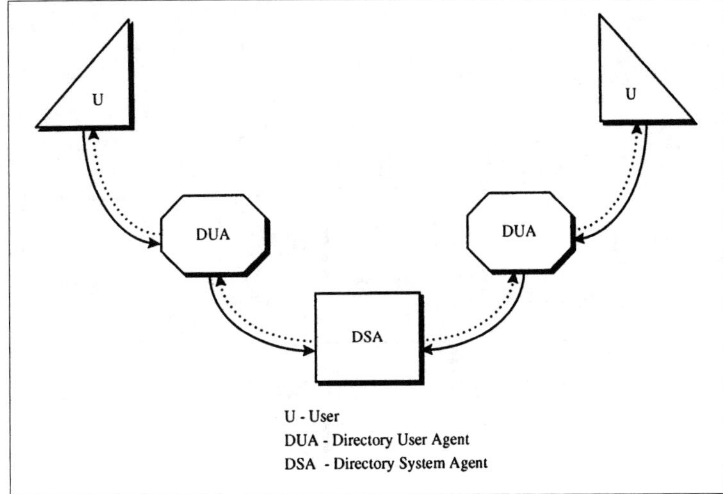

Figure 6-4. *Directory Services Model*

component called the directory user agent (DUA) that calls on the DSA to request or modify entries on behalf of the user. This is represented schematically in Figure 6-4.

Note that the DUA is a logical component and does not need to be a separate piece of software dedicated to directory access. In fact, the most common case will be that a mail UA is also a DUA. All that is necessary is for it to implement the directory look-up functions. So ALL-IN-1 3.2, for example, is considered a DUA, since it has included calls to a DSA.

While the functional diagrams of X.400 and X.500 may show some conceptual similarity, you should keep in mind that they are accomplishing different functions. So the double-headed arrows in the mail diagrams will indicate that the messages can travel in either direction. In X.500 information also travels both ways, but it is not the same type of data.

The user initiates some action to request a look-up. This might happen when a mail address has been entered and needs to be verified or when the user explicitly requests to search for a recipient. The DUA packages this request and sends it on to the DSA, which finds the

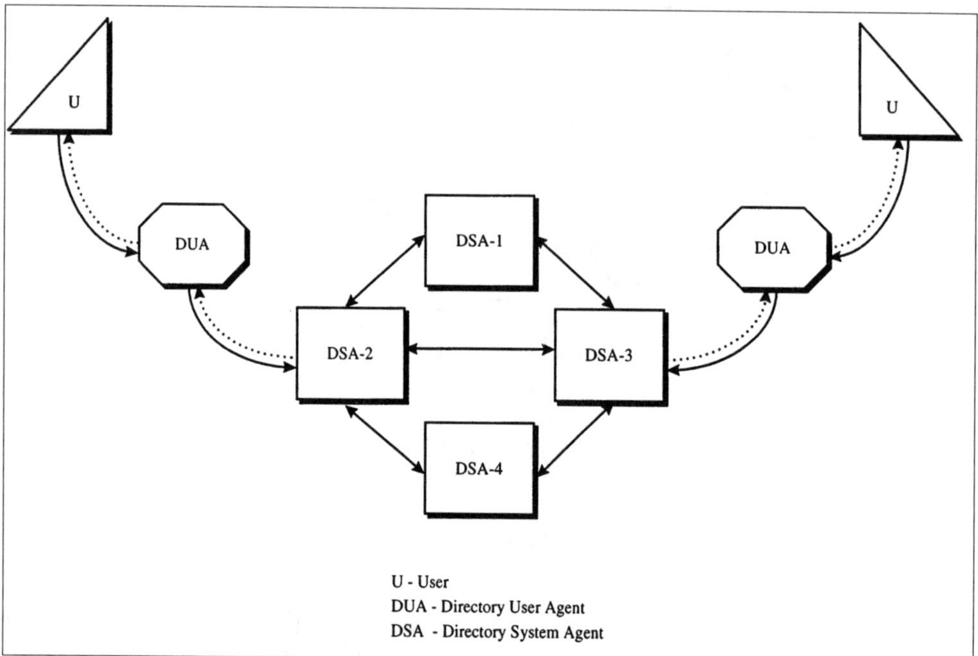

Figure 6-5. *Multiple Directory System Agents*

matching record and sends it back to the DUA and on to the user. So in one direction we have the search request and in the other the search results.

Another important implicit difference between mail submission and a directory look-up is that the look-up is synchronous. The final delivery of a mail message may not occur until after the originator has logged off and gone home. A directory search would be useless unless the user saw the results immediately.

In many cases, one DSA will be sufficient for the whole company. But in other circumstances you may want to add redundancy. Or you might have a highly distributed network with a slow link or two. It might not be ideal to have all the look-ups from the remote locations going across this bottleneck.

In this case you would want to consider employing multiple DSAs, as illustrated in Figure 6-5. All of your users could access a local DSA,

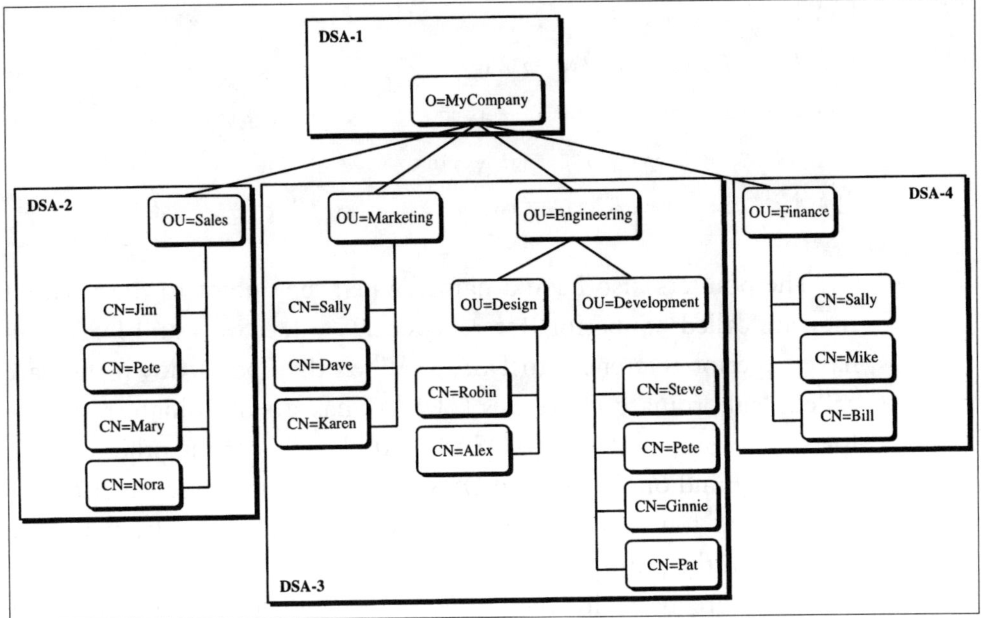

Figure 6-6. *Distributed Directory Information Tree*

and if that one has problems they could reference one of the others. X.500 directory information trees are specially designed to accommodate this type of need, but you will have to decide how you want it done (see Figure 6-6).

On the one hand, you could store only local information with each DSA and you would have a simple and fast solution. But users could not look up any of the remote entries. On the other hand, you could store all of the data with each DSA, but you would have a lot of redundant data and a very heavy network load to keep everything synchronized.

We get around this by storing local data at each node. But we don't stop there. We have pointers to the remainder of the tree so that when a user requests non-local data we can still satisfy the request by going remote.

The sections of the tree that are quartered in a particular DSA are called the naming contexts. The naming contexts for the four DSAs are:

DSA-1	`/O=MyCompany`
DSA-2	`/O=MyCompany /OU=Sales`
DSA-3	`/O=MyCompany /OU=Marketing`
	`/O=MyCompany /OU=Engineering`
DSA-4	`/O=MyCompany /OU=Finance`

The pointers also have a name. When they point to their parent they are called "Superior References." DSA-2, DSA-3 and DSA-4 all have superior references to DSA-1. When they point down they are called "subordinate references." DSA-1 has a subordinate reference for `/O=MyCompany /OU=Sales` to DSA-2 and likewise for the other naming contexts found on DSA-3 and DSA-4. If you count three superior references and four subordinate references in this example, you have understood the point.

There are basically two ways we can go about getting to the remote data. They are called chaining and referral. The main difference between them is whether it is the DUA or the DSA that goes looking for the entry.

I will continue to refer to the DIT in Figure 6-3 in the next few examples.

Chaining

In Figure 6-7 you can see an example of chaining. The user has requested a look-up, which the DUA has passed on to DSA-2. Let us assume that we are looking for Karen, in Marketing. DSA-2 is not able to find Karen, since she is not in its naming context. It knows that DSA-1 has the root entry for the Organization of MyCompany, so it should be able to find anyone underneath it, directly or indirectly. DSA-2 therefore chains to DSA-1 asking it to find Karen. DSA-1 accepts the request, but it sees that all the Marketing entries are actually managed by DSA-3, so it passes the request on to DSA-3, which returns the required information via DSA-1 and DSA-2.

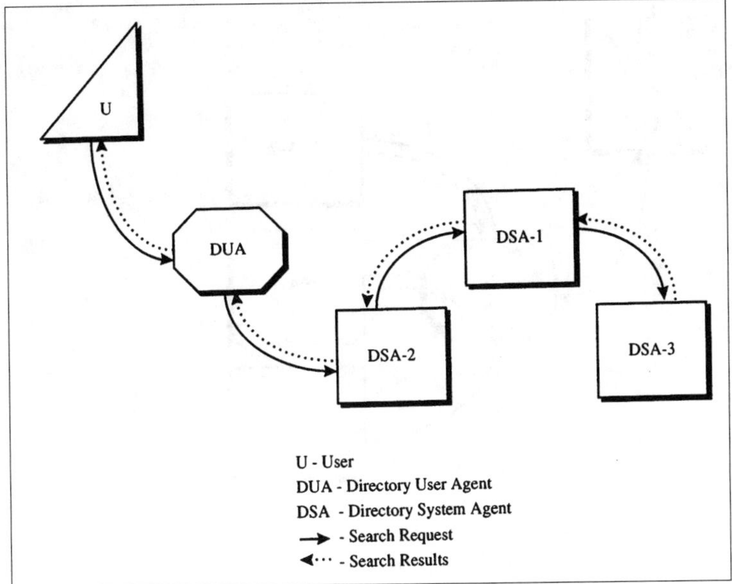

Figure 6-7. *Chaining*

Referral

Figure 6-8 illustrates the concept of referral. We again ask DSA-2 to look up Karen. It still knows that our best bet is to go to DSA-1, but this time it takes the lazy way out. Rather than looking up the information, it tells the DUA to get it itself. The DUA tries again with DSA-1, but this time it is referred to DSA-3. As you can imagine, the poor DUA is greatly relieved when DSA-3 comes back with the entry.

So why have two ways to accomplish the same thing? Chaining is easier for the DUA, but by asking the DSA to chain requests it relinquishes control. If we employ chaining, the DSAs will search until they find the entry or are sure it is nowhere in the distributed tree. This may be across some slow network links and frankly, it may just not be worth it to the user to wait that long to get the information. With a referral, there is more control closer to the user and it is possible to specify when and where to look for what.

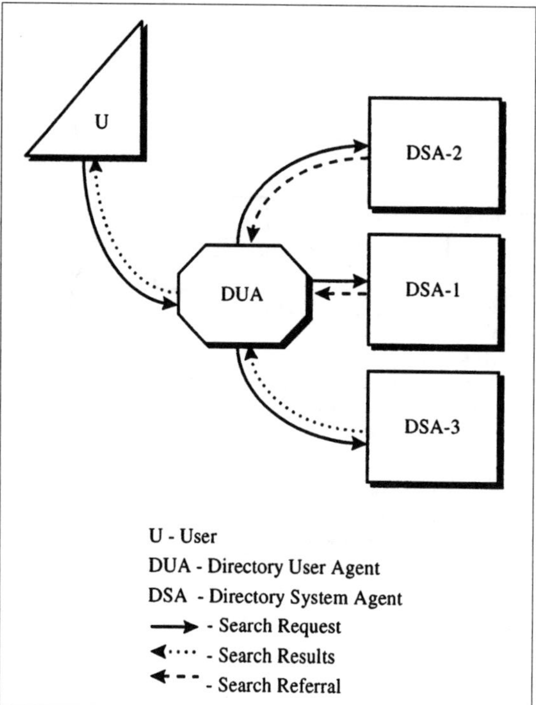

Figure 6-8. *Referral*

Shadowing

We employ links between the parts of the DIT to connect them so that we don't need to copy the data around. But sometimes we might have parts of the tree we'd like to have locally since they are accessed frequently. This is called shadowing. In Figure 6-9 we can see how DSA-1 has shadowed the data from DSAs 2, 3 and 4. Now when anyone asks for information from DSA-1 it can handle the request without chaining or referral. This has its advantages for the other DSAs, too. We now have to make at most one chaining or referral step. If we ask DSA-2 for Bill in Finance, it will chain or refer to DSA-1, and that is it. There is no more need to go to DSA-4. Shadowing can be very useful, but it also requires a great deal of directory-internal administration to keep everything synchronized. So much so that it even has its own protocols to help it out.

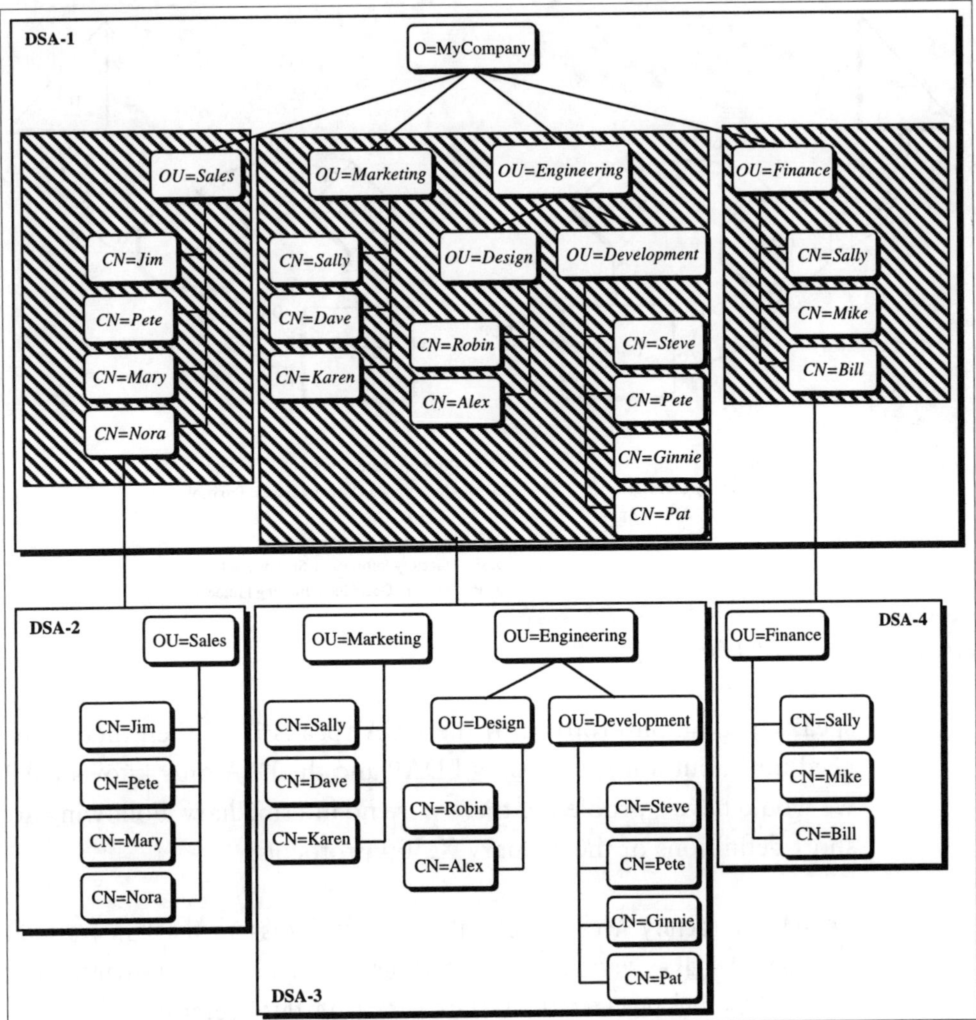

Figure 6-9. *Shadowed Directory Information Tree*

Protocols

The primary protocols used by X.500 are shown in Figure 6-10.

Note the addition of a component called a broker. It translates requests from a lightweight directory access protocol (LDAP) to a directory access protocol (DAP) in cases where neither component

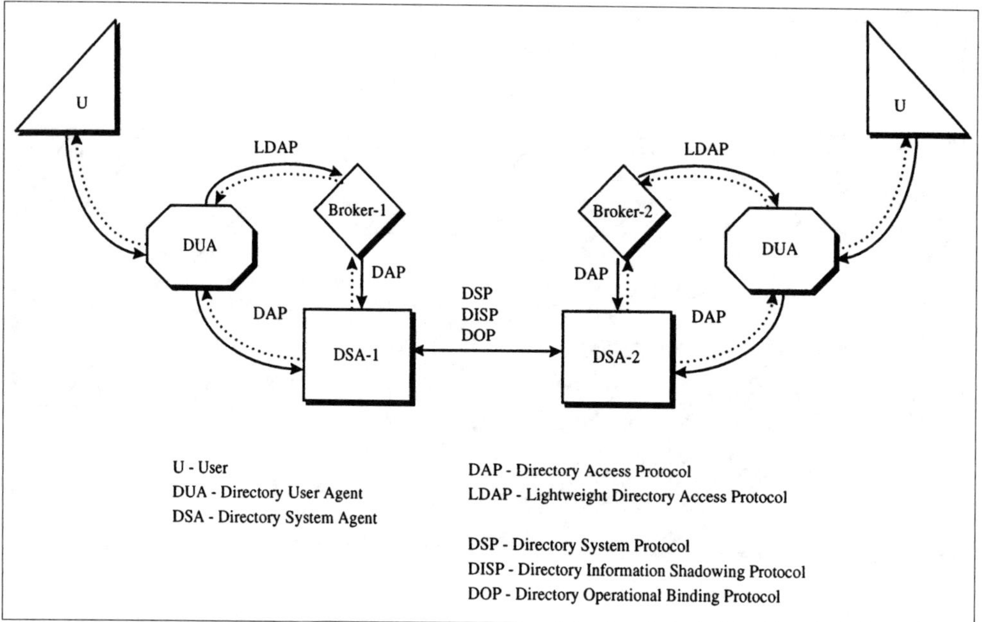

Figure 6-10. *X.500 Protocols*

speaks a common protocol. If the DUA speaks DAP then there is no need for it, but if it speaks only LDAP and the DSA only knows DAP, we would have a problem if there were no intermediary. Following are short definitions of the primary X.500 protocols:

- **DAP** (Directory Access Protocol): Defines access to the DSA from the DUA. It makes various kinds of requests (to look up information) to the DSA and receives the results back with this protocol.
- **LDAP** (Lightweight Directory Access Protocol): Since DAP has a lot of overhead and is complex to set up, someone saw an opportunity and defined RFC1777, which specifies a somewhat reduced protocol that runs over TCP/IP, is easier to set up and requires less overhead. Particularly for PCs this has become the de facto standard of DSA access, since they would otherwise be hard-pressed to use X.500 at all. We will return to LDAP later on in this chapter.
- **DSP** (Directory System Protocol): Is used between DSAs when chaining is necessary to find a requested entry.

- **DISP** (Directory Information Shadowing Protocol): Is used between DSAs to synchronize shadowed parts of the directory information tree.
- **DOP** (Directory Operational Binding Protocol): Is used between DSAs to manage operational (e.g., shadowing) agreements.

Structural Classes

I mentioned earlier that part of the difference between a directory service and a name service is the presence of additional attributes for each entry. For a person, we would typically want to define such attributes as a name, telephone number, and street address. But we also have other nodes in the tree. We have countries, for example, and we could also have localities and types of resources. It would hardly make sense to record a telephone number for these.

On the one hand, we could just define a large number of optional attributes and let people decide on their own what to enter for a particular entry. It could conceivably work, with a lot of discipline from everyone involved. Otherwise, it would be a disaster. We could have all sorts of unusable data stored all over the place, and no program would ever be able to rely on any type of consistency in the entries.

X.500 allows for the definition of structural classes. Each structural class specifies which attributes are permitted and which are required. It can even indicate what format is required for a particular attribute. Quite a number of structural classes are predefined. In our example we would have the Country, Organization, OrganizationalUnit and OrganizationalPerson, and each of these has a definition in the X.500 standard.

Note that the attributes are independent of the hierarchical structure of the tree. An entry is identified by its distinguished name, and from that its parent name is implicit. We do not need attributes to identify these. Similarly, we can browse the children of a particular entry without needing to identify them.

In addition to the required and optional attributes, we also have structure rules for the classes. It would hardly make sense to allow someone to classify an OrganizationalUnit as a subordinate of an

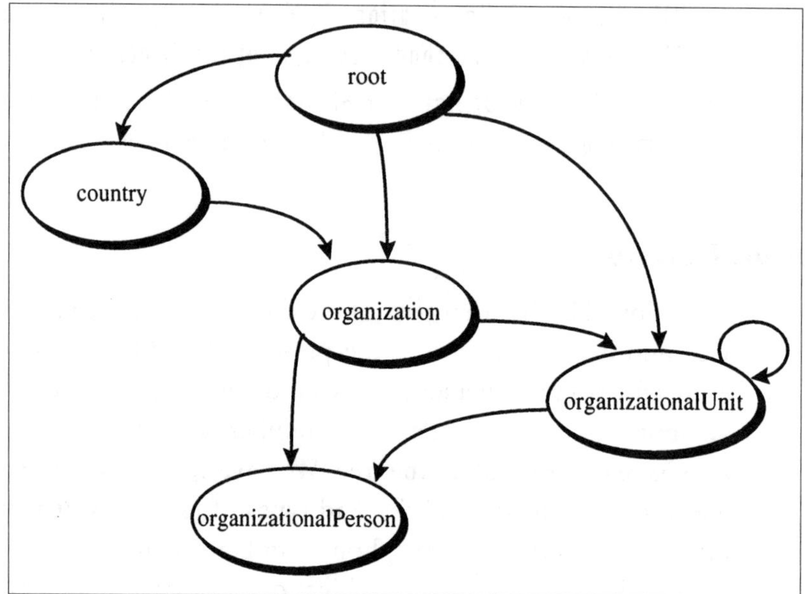

Figure 6-11. *Structure Rules*

OrganizationalPerson. But if you don't make it impossible, someone will do it sooner or later and wonder why everything isn't working. To enforce this we can define structure rules for each of the structural classes. The rules will indicate to which classes it can be subordinate. Figure 6-11 shows some of the standard structure rules. For example, in the case of OrganizationalUnit we would have a stipulation that it can only be placed under Organizations or other OrganizationalUnits. An OrganizationalPerson can fall under Organization or OrganizationalUnit.

Many of the commonly needed classes are already defined by X.500. Nevertheless, you may find that you need attributes that are not there or need to enter entirely different objects. You can define your own classes. The list of all the structural classes with all their definitions is called a schema, and you can certainly edit yours to add or modify entries.

Obviously, you need to be careful if you modify standard entries, since other applications may not deal well with your changes. The better solution is to add your own classes. If you want to describe something entirely different, you may want to start from scratch, but usually there will already be a class that is just missing the odd field. If you find one, you will want to create a subordinate class from it and simply add the fields you need.

Imagine that the OrganizationalPerson class fits you well, but you also need to have some biographical data. You could create your own BiographicalPerson. If you specify a superior class of OrganizationalPerson, you automatically inherit all its attributes and you can specify a few more like YearOfBirth, PlaceOfBirth, FathersName, MothersName, and NumberOfSiblings.

User Entries, Routing Entries and X.400 Addresses

Many people are confused by the similarity of X.400 and X.500 when it comes to specifying and managing users. The use of the X.500 directory by a mail system to store routing data on users contributes further to the potential for misunderstanding. Just in case you are one of those caught off-guard, here is a quick overview of how the two may interrelate.

As you can see in Figure 6-12, my X.500 entry is `/O=Digital /OU=AUI /CN=John Rhoton`. My X.400 address is `C=AT; A=ADA; P=Digital; O=Digital; OU=AUI; CN=John Rhoton`. Since MAILbus 400 stores the routing information in the X.500 directory, we can see both addresses in the tree. The important point is that the regular user entry gives the X.400 address, which can be used to locate the routing information in the tree.

The sequence in which these are used is as follows: Someone decides that they want to send me a message. They don't know my X.400 address, so they have the UA/DUA perform a look-up in the X.500 directory (along the left branch). It finds my entry and puts the X.400 address into the mail header. When the message is submitted to the MTA, it locates the X.400 address in the header and looks up the routing instructions in the directory (along the right branch). It sees that the user agent called UA1, which is connected to the MTA called MTA1 and is my mail application, and it routes the message accordingly.

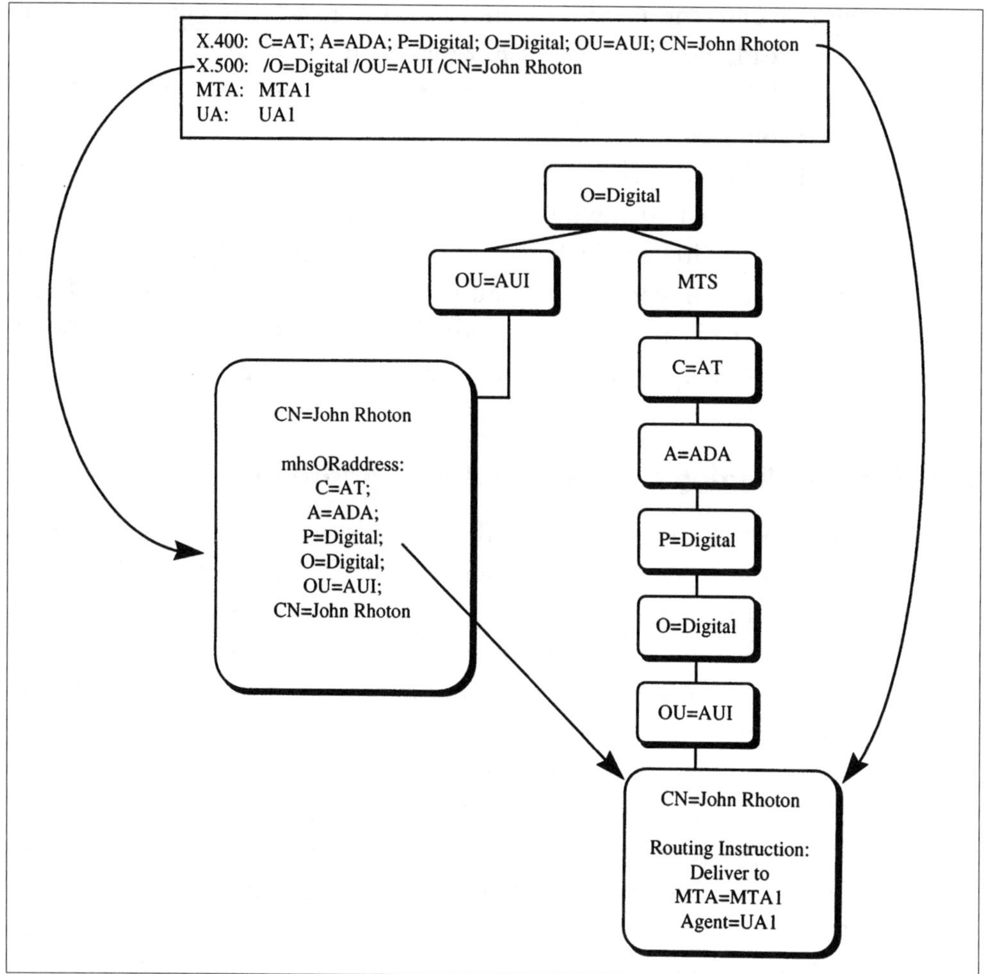

Figure 6-12. *X.400 and X.500*

X.500 and DNS

In some ways X.500 and DNS may look like competing standards:

- Both are for storing information on network-wide resources;
- Both use hierarchically structured keys for indexing information;

- Both provide similar mechanisms for distributed access and for distributing the databases themselves;
- Specifically for mail and networking, we can see that both can be and often are used for storing addressing and mail configuration information.

However, there are also some fundamental differences between the two:

- A unified DNS is in global use, whereas X.500 has many isolated directory trees;
- DNS is much simpler to implement than X.500;
- X.500 allows storage of many different types of objects; DNS has relatively few resource types;
- X.500 allows access control and requires authentication for its directory entries;
- X.500 has a much more comprehensive means of directory replication than DNS.

We could say that DNS is a streamlined distributed database with only the bare essentials to keep a network and its core applications running. X.500 is a full-fledged database meant to support almost any distributed application. It frequently contains information on the entire network's users, as well as many other objects. It therefore requires much more effort and resources to configure and manage. As a result, it is unlikely that the two will compete head to head for very many applications.

LDAP and Internet

The ITU has defined a full-fledged directory with X.500 that has no counterpart in the Internet world. There may someday be some competition, but at present there is not much activity in that area. Instead, most Internet applications have resigned to X.500 being the reigning standard.

Even though full directory protocol support, including shadowing, chaining and referrals, is not available on the Internet, that does not mean there is no need for directories. In fact, it is quite difficult to imagine a complete e-mail solution without directory support.

But instead of full directory support, the goals of the Internet are less ambitious. Almost all applications provide a personal address book of some kind, and many have a proprietary means of presenting addresses to the user from both the local system and externally defined recipients.

Nevertheless, there was a need for a standard protocol for looking up addresses on a server. This is where the lightweight directory access protocol came in. It would, of course, have been possible to just use the X.500 directory access protocol, but that is a complex protocol and many of its functions were not considered essential. The LDAP designers wanted to have a protocol that ran over TCP, so much of the session and presentation layer overhead of DAP was considered superfluous.

Simple and lightweight—these are words you hear a lot in the Internet specifications. If a protocol is to be successful it must be implemented, and the easier that is the more likely someone will do it.

LDAP servers listen for requests on TCP port 389. In contrast to many other Internet protocols, the LDAP commands are not simple text. Since the data passed is not atomic, it would be cumbersome in ASCII format. Therefore the designers of the LDAP protocol resorted to a more succinct format for passing data, similar to ASN.1. As we have seen, it is concise but not easily interpretable by humans.

Another anomaly for the TCP world is that the requests need not be answered synchronously. In other words, a client may have several outstanding requests to the same socket at any one time. The server need not answer them in order, but it should, of course, answer them eventually.

This implies a mechanism for associating responses with requests. Otherwise, clients with several outstanding requests could misinterpret the replies. To do this the clients generate a unique number (called MessageID) with each request. They pass this as part of the request, and the server returns it with any associated responses. In addition to this MessageID, one of several requests or responses is specified, as shown in Table 6-1.

Table 6-1. *LDAP Requests and Responses*

Requests	Responses
BindRequest	BindResponse
UnbindRequest	
SearchRequest	SearchResponse
ModifyRequest	ModifyResponse
AddRequest	AddResponse
DelRequest	DelResponse
ModifyRDNRequest	ModifyRDNResponse
CompareRequest	CompareResponse
AbandonRequest	

"BindRequest" initiates a session and provides any required authentication to the server. This session remains open until the client generates an "UnbindRequest" to terminate it.

By far the most common action performed by an LDAP client is a search for an entry in the directory. This is accomplished by a "SearchRequest," which specifies such items as the root of the search and its scope as well as the search criteria. The LDAP server performs the search in the directory and then returns a series of responses, one for each matching entry.

We can also use LDAP to "Modify," "Add" and "Delete" objects in the directory information base. Or we may modify the distinguished name of an entry. To do this we may modify only the last related distinguished name of any particular branch, so a full change of a DN may require the superior branches to also be modified.

"CompareRequests" allow us to ascertain whether an entry has a specific attribute. While it would be possible to perform a search to obtain the same information, this method is much more concise.

The server is under no constraint to answer requests in any particular order and may actually require a significant amount of time to handle some operations. It is possible that during this time the client has proceeded to another function and no longer needs the response originally solicited. Both for efficiency and simplicity of code, there is therefore an "AbandonRequest" option.

As you can see, LDAP provides most of what you would normally need to access from a mail client. And since it does this with relative simplicity, a number of e-mail clients have incorporated the protocol, making it the de facto standard for directory access.

Highlights

- X.500 is the only accepted international standard for a directory service.
- DNS is similar in concept but lends itself to different purposes.
- Internet mail clients may access X.500 directories using LDAP.
- LDAP is an Internet protocol, but not a typical one (terse structure and asynchronous operation).

References

Albitz, Paul, and C. Liu. 1992. *DNS and BIND*. Sebastopol, CA: O'Reilly and Associates. ISBN 1-56592-010-4.

Chadwick, David. 1996. *Understanding X.500: The Directory*. International Thomson Computer Press. ISBN 1-85032-281-3.

Yeong, W., et al. 1995. *Lightweight Directory Access Protocol* (RFC 1777).

Chapter 7

Security

System Security

It is a good thing to trust others, but sometimes it is even better not to trust. The question is when to be wary and when to accept what you receive at face value. Ideally you will not have to make that decision; the system will perform all of the security checking for you. But that leads you to the next question: Can you trust the system?

There are various ways of classifying computers in terms of how much security they provide. The best known and most widely used way is the Trusted Computer Standards Evaluation Criteria (the Orange Book) from the U.S. Department of Defense. They have defined a number of levels of security and certify the levels met by different operating systems.

Table 7-1. *Security Levels from the Orange Book*

Level	Description
D1	No protection
C1	Logon identification; file and directory permissions
C2	Authorization levels; audit trail
B1	Multilevel security; mandatory access controls
B2	Structured protection — interaction between objects at different security levels
B3	Security domains enforced by hardware
A	Verified design — mathematically verified security architecture

In Table 7-1 you can see a rough overview of the kinds of protection the various DOD security levels enforce. While you will typically not want to use a completely unprotected machine (except maybe at home), you are also unlikely to require anything as ambitious as levels A or even B. That is, unless you are paranoid or have a stock of nuclear weapons you don't want your enemies to know about.

This means that you will very likely have someone, like a system administrator, who is able to access your files to perform such mundane tasks as backing them up, monitoring disk usage, or even cleaning up your account should you ever depart. These people are usually very busy and have much more important things to do then play pranks with your e-mail. Usually; almost always! But is that enough?

There is another problem when it comes to securing e-mail: It isn't enough for my system to be secure. If I send you a message, and my system is the most secure in the world, but yours is completely open, what good does it do either of us? We can work around that; we will put a secure operating system on your machine. But what about all of those machines that are routing the message from my computer to yours? What if they intercept a couple of packets and replace a few words or numbers? E-mail is a networked application, so we need to look at the security of the network before we even begin to think about having a secure e-mail environment.

E-mail Security

I don't know the main purpose of your e-mail. It could be just chatting with a remote colleague, or something more important, like conducting a business transaction, discussing troop movements or planning a criminal activity. But regardless of your use, you will always have a common set of concerns regarding security of your e-mail. The only factor that varies is how important it is to you to have this security.

Let us take a look at what secure e-mail involves.

Privacy and Encryption

When you write a message you typically know who will be reading it. You can put them on your distribution list and they will receive the mail. But how would you feel if someone else took the liberty to scan through your mail messages without your permission? It would be a violation of your privacy. Depending on the message and who read it, it may or may not be critical but, in principle, most of us take no delight in the thought of others monitoring or intercepting our mail. The most common approach to guaranteeing privacy is to encrypt the message. This implies that only those who have the appropriate key to decrypt the message will be able to read its contents.

Authentication or Non-repudiation

Imagine that you receive a message from your boss asking you to book the next flight to Rio de Janeiro and spend a couple of weeks with a new customer, the Copacabana Beachside Resort. If you have some spare time you might find the thought attractive. But what if the mail didn't really come from your boss, but instead came from a malicious hacker whose chances of promotion you are blocking!

When you get messages, you don't want to have to call up every time and verify that they were sent by the persons listed as their authors. The system should be able to establish that for you. But, especially in a networked environment, this is not always as easy as it may sound.

The counterpart of authentication is non-repudiation. An example of this would be if someone sent an insulting message around the network or to selected targets and then, after sobering up, decided that hadn't been such a good idea. It would be convenient to just claim that the message was forged, but we must all take responsibility for our actions, and non-repudiation rigidly enforces this ethical principle.

Integrity

Now let's take the authentication issue one step further. You receive a message from your supplier confirming your order and providing you with a bank account number to make the payment. You have some good e-mail software, so you know that it really did come from the supplier—but just to be sure, you call up your contact and ask for confirmation. Yes, they sent the message, so you can go ahead and ask your bank to make the transfer.

But what you don't know is that your network provider employs a dubious programmer. He has a bad habit that consists of intercepting mail messages passing through his machine and making a couple of changes. In your case, these included the bank account number.

The good news is that he is about to kick the habit (when he absconds with your money). The bad news is that your boss has no sense of humor.

Approaches to Security

There are really two ways to provide secure e-mail service. The first approach is to check each link on the path from the source to the destination and make sure it is safe. The second approach is to provide additional facilities to both the sender and the receiver to ensure that they have a secure path between them.

Network Security

A secure network is one in which each connection is guaranteed. If my machine has a link to another machine, I know for certain that it is really that other machine on the line. I also know that there is no way for anyone else to monitor or interfere with our connection, either because we have performed some encryption on the line or simply because we have a physically distinct cable. If I know that the mail applications on both ends are safe and all the links between them are too, then I can assume a certain amount about the message transfer.

Application-Based Security

If our network is not secure enough for us to depend on it, we have to resort to other measures. The most likely means of doing this is to build the security into the messaging application at both ends or, alternatively, to make use of an additional piece of software to provide privacy and integrity.

X.400 Security

The messaging model of X.400 has everything it needs to provide security; that does not, however, mean that everything is always used. To begin with, an X.400 network is rigidly secure. To connect to a message transfer agent, a user agent or another message transfer agent must:

1. Be registered with the destination MTA;
2. Reside on the network address where it is registered;
3. Supply a password that is also registered with the destination MTA.

If the underlying network is X.25, we have the additional security that it provides in guaranteeing network addresses.

This, however, does not prohibit someone from tampering with one of the UAs, or even the MTAs, on their way through the network. The messages are transmitted in ASN.1 format, so it is not an easy chore, but it can be done.

Clearly, any kind of security in the application would need to be coordinated with the UAs. And each source UA needs to have a way of telling the destination UAs which security mechanism is being used for a particular message. Here theory and practice diverge once again. You can use an object identifier to specify your encryption, but no one has actually bothered to ensure that the identifiers be globally registered. As a result, you can implement a proprietary convention, but you cannot be sure that external correspondents will adhere to the same convention.

X.509

X.509 is a draft ITU–T standard that deserves some mention. Ironically, it looks like the Internet community may use it more than other ITU groups. I will discuss it later, when I talk about public keys and certification authorities.

Internet Security

The Internet uses a different paradigm when it comes to connecting computers and networks. Rather than the rigid structure provided by X.25, we have machines connecting all over the place to a loosely controlled network. The protocols are meant to be simple and don't bother with making a lot of checks. Instead, it is up to you to protect your machine if you think there is cause.

Firewalls

And if you look at the Internet at large, I am sure you will agree that there is cause. It doesn't take many hackers to make your data vulnerable. But within an organization, the situation is often different. It is possible to monitor what is happening and check both the computers and the lines between them. What is needed is simply a means of keeping intruders out of the internal network while still allowing your users access to the Internet and all it has to offer.

The typical answer to this need is a firewall, or screening router (see Figure 7-1). It intercepts every packet going in or out of the internal network and checks to see if it should let it through. By giving the firewall a set of rules, it is possible to restrict either incoming or outgoing access to a set of applications.

Table 7-2 gives an example of rules we could set up for our firewall. We could tell it to allow incoming requests to port 80 (HTTP) of our Web server and port 25 (SMTP) of our mail server, but to disallow all others. We could also tell it that we want to allow all internal users access to port 80 (HTTP) on external systems, but that only our mail server should be able to make direct SMTP connections outside.

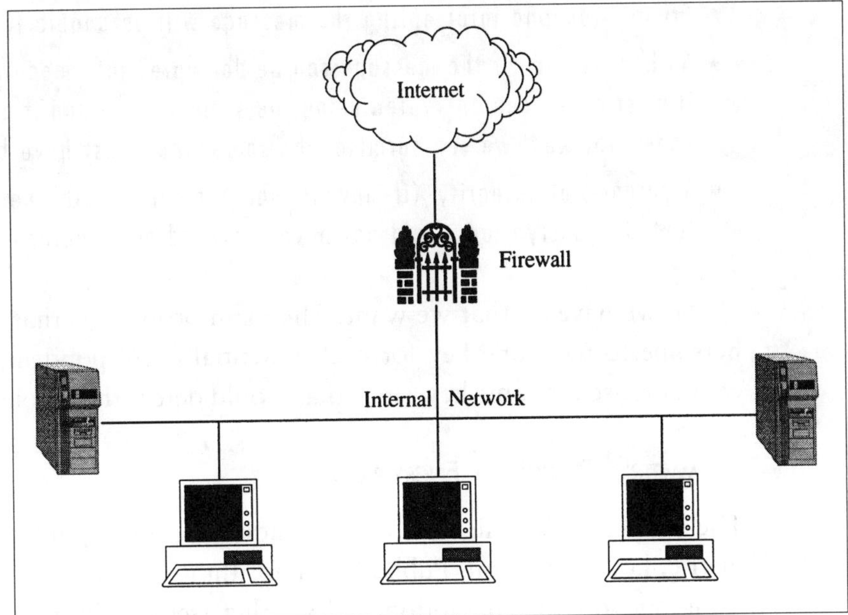

Figure 7-1. *Internet Firewall*

Table 7-2. *Simplified Firewall Rules*

Incoming Port	Incoming Address	Outgoing Port	Outgoing Address
*	*	TCP:80	www.myco.com
*	*	TCP:25	mail.myco.com
*	*.myco.com	TCP:80	*
*	mail.myco.com	TCP:25	*

Encrypting and Certifying Mail

Symmetric Key Encryption

The simplest form of mail encryption involves what is known as a symmetrical, or private, key. Both the sender and receiver have the same key, which one has given to the other. The sender encrypts the message using this key, sends it on its way, and at the other end the recipient decrypts the message using the same key. If nobody else has access to the key and the algorithm is sound, then we have achieved:

- Privacy (anyone intercepting the message will be unable to read it);
- Authentication (if the message can be decrypted into meaningful text, it must have been encrypted using the same key — and if no one else knows the key, we can surmise who the sender must have been);
- Assurance of integrity (if anyone had tampered with the encrypted text, the decryption would not have produced meaningful text).

So we have all that we want. The main problem is that it is cumbersome to have one key for each potential correspondent. But you cannot reuse the same key, since that would defeat the whole purpose.

Asymmetric (Public) Key Encryption

The answer to this dilemma is a technique known as public, or asymmetric, key encryption. Public key algorithms have the distinction of using one key for encryption and another (seemingly unrelated) key for decryption. It is important to realize that decryption works only with the *second* key. What this means is that it is possible to freely distribute one of your keys (the public key), while keeping the other one (the private key) top-secret. This gives you two options, which can be combined:

1. You can sign a message by encrypting it with your private key. Others will be able to decrypt it with your public key, and they will know both that the message has come from you (authenticity) and that it cannot have been altered since the time you encrypted it (integrity).
2. You can encrypt a message with your recipient's public key. Since only she has the corresponding private key, nobody else will be able to decrypt (and thus read) the message in transit.

It is much more difficult to write algorithms for public key encryption than for private key encryption. You can imagine that it isn't that difficult to write a program to encrypt and decrypt data using the same key. But try to imagine how to write a routine that encrypts using one key and decrypts using another that is not visible to the first! It almost seems impossible, but fortunately, cryptographers have managed to find some mathematical functions that do the job effectively. The idea originated with two researchers at Stanford University named Whitfield Diffie and Martin Hellman. In 1976 they invented a means of public key cryptography called the Diffie-Hellman Exponential Key Exchange. This approach was taken further by three professors at MIT named Ronald Rivest, Adi Shamir and Len Adleman, who patented an algorithm called RSA, which is the base of most current public key encryption.

The main drawback to public key encryption is that it tends to have more involved algorithms, which take longer to encrypt and decrypt. This factor needs to be balanced against the need for tighter security.

Certification Authorities

Public keys provide for encryption as well as providing a means of ensuring authenticity of origin and integrity of content. It is also much easier to distribute one public key than a host of private ones. But it is still not ideal. What would be your normal means of letting a group of people know your public key? You could mail it to them, but that defeats the whole purpose. How can I prevent someone else from impersonating me and sending out a bogus public key?

Administering public keys is the role of a certification authority. It guarantees that a given public key belongs to a certain individual, so I can be confident that it corresponds to that person's private key.

Of course, administering this set-up is not trivial. It requires us to have a means of identifying people uniquely. We also must have a way to ensure that someone registering a public key is really who she says she is.

While it may be difficult to coordinate a large directory of users and their keys, the need is growing by the day. The possibility of electronic commerce being conducted via the Internet makes the need more pronounced. With million-dollar transactions being performed electronically, we need to ensure that people are who they say they are.

The best known attempt at this is described in X.509, "The Directory-Authentication Framework." But this standard only describes how certificates should look so that the validating software can use them. We still need organizations that will function as the authorities. There are currently a couple of services offered, but commercial opportunities may well entice others onto the playing field in the coming years. At present, both a new company called VeriSign and the U.S. Postal Service plan to offer their services in the market.

MIME and Security

While MIME did not address security from the onset, there have been newer RFCs that specify how it can accommodate various encryption and signature algorithms. In particular, RFC 1847 defines security multiparts that can be either signed or encrypted. These are similar to the standard MIME bodyparts, but they differ in a couple of respects. The protocol (encryption algorithm) must be specified, as well as the message integrity check algorithm (micalg). The signed bodyparts must also come in pairs (i.e., the text and the signature).

PGP

A cryptographer named Phil Zimmerman developed a piece of software called PGP (Pretty Good Privacy). It has been the subject of some controversy, since it used the RSA algorithm without clear agreement from its owners, and also because the software made its way around the world, which upset the U.S. government. Nevertheless, due in large part to its free distribution, it is probably the most widespread cryptographic software in the world.

PGP (like all commercially viable software) uses both symmetrical and asymmetrical keys to perform its encryption. This provides the security of public keys while at the same time reducing the processing time for encryption. PGP generates a random session key, which it encrypts with RSA. It then uses the encrypted session key and IDEA (a symmetrical algorithm) to encrypt the actual message.

An interesting point about PGP is its approach to certification. Rather than relying on a central authority, the PGP model uses a web of trust. Briefly, the way this works is that you are able to certify specific keys as belonging to the person declared. In addition, you can indicate whether or not (or to what extent) you trust other people. If you trust them, you will also accept any keys they have certified.

What this means is that, assuming that people are relatively generous with their trust, you will eventually trust the people they have trusted and gradually amass a large number of validated keys. It is not too difficult to imagine how this works on a small scale, and it seems to work even in communities of several thousand users. However, it is questionable whether this approach can be applied worldwide, particularly when dealing with messages of critical importance.

RFC 2015 defines how to support PGP encryption and signatures within MIME. Leaning on RFC 1847, it defines the PGP algorithms as protocols "application/pgp-encrypted" and "application/pgp-signature," respectively, and provides some additional syntactic specifications for the PGP text.

PEM

While PGP is largely the work of one man, PEM (privacy enhanced mail) and the other algorithms described here are actually Internet standards. PEM is specified in RFCs 1421 through 1424. Like PGP, it uses RSA to encrypt the keys and uses a symmetric key for actual message encryption. It uses DES rather than IDEA.

PEM's main drawback is that it supports only seven-bit ASCII. (It predates the MIME specification.) It is also very stringent in imposing the need to use digital certificates, implying a central authority. While this may often be acceptable, it deters small groups of users.

PEM does not have a large market presence and has little chance of competing with PGP and S/MIME.

MOSS

MOSS (MIME object-oriented security services) was designed to overcome the limitations of PEM. It is able to accommodate MIME messages and various algorithms and does not require a certification authority. Unfortunately, while it is considered a good technical solution, it has very little support in the marketplace.

S/MIME

Most people see the future of encrypted mail as belonging to S/MIME (secure/multipurpose Internet mail extensions). It is supported by RSA and uses their PKCS (public-key cryptography standards) numbers seven and ten, for key encryption and certification, respectively. It is not yet an Internet standard, but it looks likely that it will be formalized as an RFC soon.

With S/MIME, the actual message encryption can be done with DES, Triple-DES and RC2, all of which are symmetric encryption algorithms.

Several points are helping to tilt the balance in favor of S/MIME:

- S/MIME scales well;
- A public domain implementation is planned;
- It supports Digital certificates (obtainable from VeriSign);
- Tools are available for building S/MIME clients in the market;
- S/MIME is designed to work with MIME from the outset;
- PKCS is embedded in a number of software packages.

Highlights

- X.400 offers a more secure messaging backbone.
- X.400 offers facilities (but no implementation) for secure mail messages.
- X.509 is the recognized standard for a certification authority.
- SMTP has RFCs for several different encryption algorithms.
- PGP is the predominant encryption program in use at present.
- S/MIME appears to be the future direction of message encryption.

References

Balenson, D. 1993. *Privacy Enhancement for Internet Electronic Mail: Part III: Algorithms, Modes, and Identifiers* (RFC 1423).

Chapman, D. Brent, and Elizabeth D. Zwicky. 1995. *Building Internet Firewall.* O'Reilly and Associates. ISBN 1-56592-124-0.

Crocker, S., et al. 1995. *MIME Object Security Services* (RFC 1848).

Elkins, M. 1996. *MIME Security with Pretty Good Privacy (PGP)* (RFC 2015).

Galvin, J., et al. 1995. *Security Multiparts for MIME: Multipart/Signed and Multipart/Encrypted* (RFC 1847).

Garfinkel, S. 1995. *PGP: Pretty Good Privacy.* O'Reilly and Associates. ISBN 1-56592-098-8.

Hare, Chris, and K. Siyan. 1996. *Internet Firewalls and Network Security*. New Riders. ISBN 1-56205-632-8.

Kaliski, B. 1993. *Privacy Enhancement for Internet Electronic Mail: Part IV: Key Certification and Related Services* (RFC 1424).

Kent, S. 1993. *Privacy Enhancement for Internet Electronic Mail: Part II: Certificate-Based Key Management* (RFC 1422).

Linn, J. 1993. *Privacy Enhancement for Internet Electronic Mail: Part I: Message Encryption and Authentication Procedures* (RFC 1421).

Chapter 8

Heterogeneous Mail Networks

Other Messaging Backbones

In past years a number of companies experimented with departmental implementations of various mail systems. Although this was a good first step, the use of mail has become increasingly important, and it has been necessary to link an array of disparate applications together. This has turned out to be a formidable task.

We can distinguish, somewhat arbitrarily, between three kinds of mail systems:

1. Traditional corporate e-mail systems. These robust backbones were developed for large-scale enterprise use. They are primarily host-based, often with a terminal interface available. Now sometimes seen as legacy applications, although their interfaces and functionality are continuously being improved. Examples in this category might include PROFS, ALL-IN-1 and OpenMail.
2. Primarily LAN-based. Files reside on PC file services, often called post offices. Several users are assigned to each post office and access those files directly. Dedicated programs run to transfer mail from one post office to another. Examples in this category include cc:Mail or Microsoft Mail.
3. Client-server. The current leadership in the market belongs to a set of products that work exclusively in client-server mode. They address the

corporate needs for robustness and security while at the same time offering end-users the functionality and intuitive interface of the PC. They support the necessary protocols to function as their own backbone and to connect to a variety of other mail systems and backbones. Lotus Notes and Microsoft Exchange are the market leaders in this category.

As opposed to mail applications, X.400 and SMTP can be considered messaging backbones. By this we mean that they provide a mechanism for delivering messages from one mail application to another. They are the primary, but by no means the only, backbones in use today. Later in the chapter we will look at what is entailed in connecting two heterogeneous mail networks. But before we do that, it would be useful to provide a cursory overview of the architecture of these other backbones.

In some ways the backbones are necessarily similar, since they provide the same functionality. But in others they differ, and this is what we need to watch when we connect them. Some of the features we can look at are ones we have already covered in our discussion of X.400 and SMTP:

- What network protocols do they support?
- How does the addressing syntax look?
- What routing topologies do they use?
- What message format and bodypart types do they have?
- Are there any directory services available for them?

Message Router

MAILbus (without 400) was Digital's primary mail backbone for many years before MAILbus 400 came along. It was used to connect ALL-IN-1 and MailWorks, as well as supporting a number of gateways to other mail systems. The main MAILbus component was Message Router, which was essentially an MTA. In addition, it was possible to add several gateways, as well as directory services and event reporting. While "the MAILbus set" might be a more accurate term to describe this approach, I refer to it as Message Router to avoid confusion with the MAILbus 400 products. If you haven't encountered Message Router yet, you probably never will. It is being replaced by X.400 and SMTP backbones as I write. My main reason for including it is to give you a historical perspective on backbones and to show an alternate approach to backbone architecture.

DECnet Phase IV

Message Router was developed at a time when Digital was running DECnet Phase IV. In contrast to DECnet Phase V, which is OSI compliant, this version encompassed a set of mainly proprietary protocols.

Message Router Topology

As you can see in Figure 8-1, the main distinction in the topology is a difference in terminology, in that the components doing the work of a message transfer agent are called message routers.

In terms of openness, Message Router supports both a closed and an open topology. Similar to SMTP, it is possible to configure a message router to accept connections from any other DECnet machine and to forward mail to any other DECnet machine. Alternately, it is possible, as with X.400, to restrict message traffic to a specific set of nodes on the network.

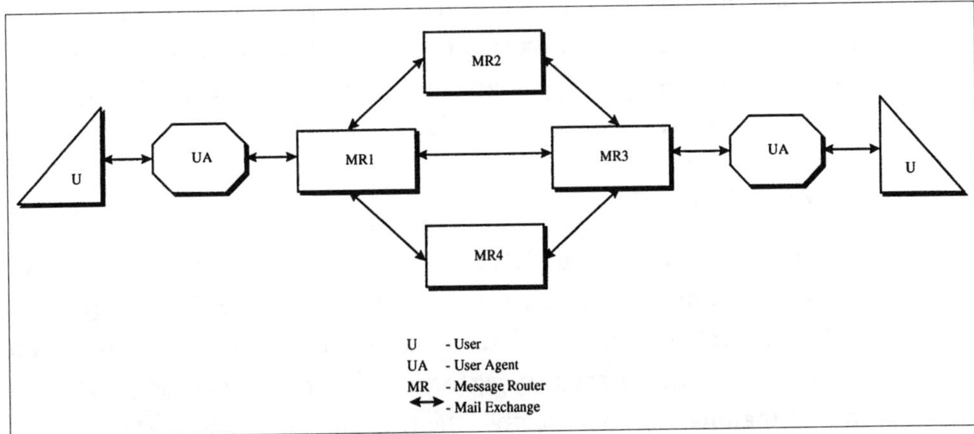

Figure 8-1. *MAILbus*

Route-Based Addressing

In contrast to X.400, Message Router requires explicit routing in the address. This means that if a particular message router does not know a user, we must explicitly tell it where to route the message.

In the scenario above the user on the left could therefore address the user on the right as

```
User2 @ MR3 @ MR1
```

or alternatively as

```
User2 @ MR3 @ MR2 @ MR1
```

or as

```
User2 @ MR3 @ MR4 @ MR1
```

This type of addressing has the disadvantage that a person's address is dependent on the location of the originator. It is possible to universalize the addressing in a particular network, but this requires that all message routers have entries for all other message routers or some even more complex configuration.

Message Format

Message Router stores messages in a format called NBS, which was specified by the National Bureau of Standards. It allows attachments, but these may only be added sequentially. There is no support for a hierarchical bodypart structure like in X.400 or MIME. The files may be binary or of any file type. However, they must be tagged with a recognized message router tag when they are submitted.

Directory Support

MAILbus did not support X.500 or even LDAP. It did, however, have something similar called distributed directory services (DDS). You can define a number of user entries, called subscribers, and enter their mail addresses so that users can perform look-ups on remote addressees rather than having to remember their actual addresses.

Microsoft Exchange

Microsoft Exchange is the newest addition to corporate mail backbones. The product is the successor to Microsoft Mail, but it is a complete rewrite of the LAN-based e-mail system, tailored to large corporate needs.

The architecture of Exchange is that of a three-tiered mail system:

1. User interface (client);
2. Mail server (server);
3. Mail backbone.

Exchange offers functionality for all three tiers, which can be used together or in conjunction with any other compatible applications.

In Exchange, the client communicates with the server using MAPI (or mail application programming interface). This means that other MAPI clients can connect to the Exchange server or, vice versa, that the Exchange client can connect to other MAPI service providers. This independence makes it easy for third parties to offer additional functionality that complements Exchange.

As we shall see, Exchange is also able to function as a backbone. However, it is equally capable of using another backbone (e.g., X.400 or SMTP) if one is in place.

I will not spend too much time on the architecture of the Exchange server, since it is well described in the industry literature.[1] For our purposes we need only to clarify some terminology.

Exchange stores all the messages in a set of files called the information store. The server-based documents can be shared (public folders) or exclusively assigned (private folders). Additionally, there is the option of client-only (personal folders) and synchronized (offline folders) documents stored on the user's desktop.

When a user sends a message, a process called the MTA takes the message from the information store, looks up the recipient(s) and

---

1 See Redmond (1997) for a good overview of Microsoft Exchange V5.0 in terms of architecture, planning and design.

gives it to the relevant connectors. These connectors actually transfer the message to another system.

Network Protocols

Exchange offers support for several of the LAN-based protocols for client-server communication. For connections between MTAs, it is possible to use TCP/IP or X.25.

Exchange Topology

Microsoft Exchange is a messaging application. As such, it covers all of the functionality of a user agent. But it can also connect to various backbones and other Exchange servers to transfer mail to remote users.

To connect with a remote site an Exchange server must have a connector installed. The connector provides the protocols and format supported across a particular communication channel.

The Enterprise edition of the Microsoft Exchange server offers four standard connectors for backbone use (see Figure 8-2). These connectors can be installed in any combination. The following are short descriptions of the connectors:

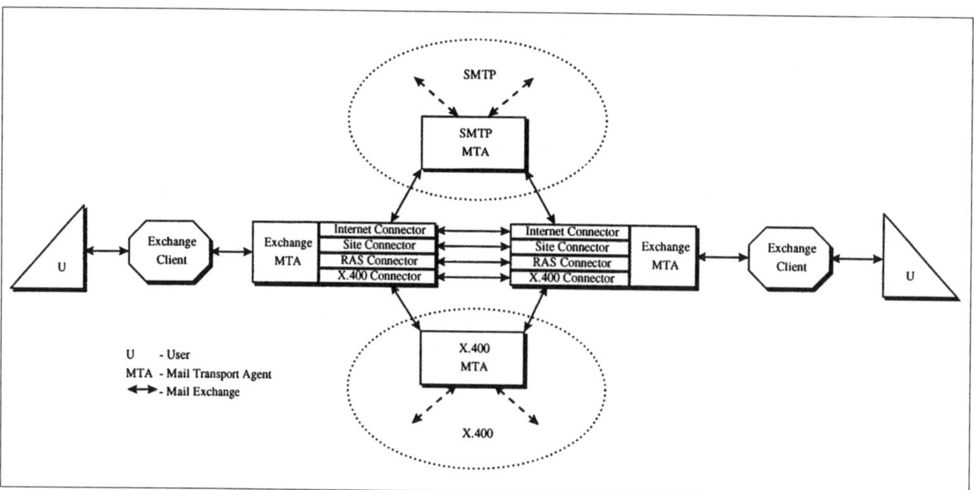

Figure 8-2. *Exchange Connectors*

- **Site connector**: LAN connection with another Exchange server using remote procedure calls (RPCs).
- **RAS connector**: Remote access service (RAS) connection to another Exchange server across a dial-up line.
- **Internet connector**: SMTP connection to another Exchange server or any IP node.
- **X.400 connector**: X.400 connection between Exchange servers or to an X.400 network.

Beyond these, you also have standard connectors to link up to other mail systems like cc:Mail or Microsoft Mail. And there are numerous third-party connectors for diverse mail systems and other non-mail devices like fax or telex.

Of most interest for connecting Exchange sites is the X.400 connector. It offers good performance, as well as significant control in terms of scheduling and access restrictions.

It can be configured to use one of three transport stacks:

- TP0/X.25 with an Eicon port adapter;
- TCP/IP using RFC 1006;
- TP4/CLNP across a local area network.

Note that Exchange is not only able to connect to other backbones such as X.400 and SMTP. It can also function as its own backbone. Initially, this means that you can connect several Exchange systems together, using any of the connectors without any external backbone.

But beyond this, it means that mail can be routed through Exchange from one external mail system to another. It would be possible, for example, to send X.400 mail to the Internet by placing an appropriately configured Exchange server between the backbones. As you can see depicted in Figure 8-3, Exchange is capable of forming a link between various mail systems and backbones such as Microsoft Mail, X.400 or SMTP, thus enabling all of the users in the mail network to communicate with each other.

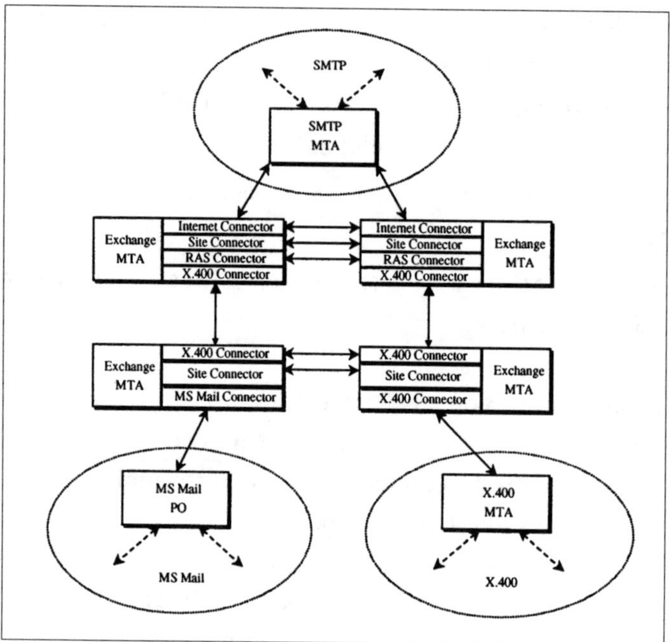

Figure 8-3. *Microsoft Exchange As a Backbone*

Addressing

Exchange offers different addressing formats, depending on the intended recipient. If the message is to be sent via the X.400 connector, the address will be entered in that format. Similarly, if it is going to SMTP or Microsoft Mail, the address must be specified using the appropriate syntax. For addressees who are Exchange users in the same Exchange organization, be they on the same server or not, the addressing format is Exchange's own X.500-like syntax.

The number of different addressing formats and possible connectors is a source of potential confusion. There is obviously a need to map the various addresses to the appropriate connectors so that the messages can be delivered correctly. Defining address spaces does this. An address space is a partial address (e.g., `c=IE;a=Eirmail400;p=Digital;o=Digital`) mapped to a particular connection. All messages destined to recipients containing the partial address (e.g., `c=IE;a=Eirmail400;p=Digital;o=Digital;s=rhoton;g=john`) will be routed to the connection.

All of the address spaces are consolidated and coordinated with the configuration of the other servers in the Exchange organization to produce a set of routing instructions. Each server maintains these in a routing table called the GWART (gateway address routing table). Fortunately, these calculations are largely made automatically, and the mail managers need not go though the laborious task of updating them each time a change is made to the configuration or topology. What is interesting about Exchange in this respect is that the addresses are largely transparent to the users. All users in the organization, as well as any external recipients who have been manually entered, can be found in the global address list. These addresses appear with the common name of the user. The full addresses are not normally displayed on the mail message.

Message Format

Exchange supports the various formats used by its connectors. Both internally and between Exchange sites, it stores messages in an internal (proprietary) format, but it performs any necessary conversion before sending the messages on to the outside. In any case, the internal format is able to accommodate a hierarchical bodypart structure with the various PC formats that are typically used in an Exchange environment.

Directory

Exchange uses an X.500-like directory implementation. It is not fully compliant, as it does not yet support the X.500 protocols, such as DAP and DSP. In Exchange V5.0 there is, however, support for LDAP. This means that it is possible for users to look up Exchange addresses from the Exchange server using any LDAP client.

Since the current version of Exchange does not support the X.500 protocol suite, they must use their own mechanism to allow access to directory information throughout the organization. This is done by replication. When Exchange servers are connected to each other, they broadcast all the directory changes to each other, thus ensuring that all Exchange servers know of the recipients of all the other Exchange servers.

Lotus Notes

It would be interesting to compare the functionality of Lotus Notes to Microsoft Exchange, as they appear to be the main e-mail players for the years to come. However, their functionality goes beyond providing mail backbones into a number of different groupware and workflow functions, which are beyond the scope of this book.

When it comes to mail architecture, there is actually similarity in their designs, although the terminology may be slightly different. Similar to Exchange, Lotus Notes also offers the facility to provide X.400 and SMTP connections. Rather than call these processes connectors, they are called MTAs. These components are optional with Lotus Notes and provide not only a means of connecting to a foreign e-mail system, but also, similarly to Exchange, a means to connect to other Lotus Notes systems. Lotus offers four main MTAs:

- Notes Mail (for Notes–Notes connections; akin to the site connector in Exchange);
- SMTP/MIME;
- X.400;
- cc:Mail.

IBM PROFS

PROFS (Professional Office System) was released by IBM in the mid-1980s and has made its mark, particularly in corporations with large user communities. It allowed for very large single-server installations (over 50 thousand users on a single system), which meant that its need for connectivity was reduced. Since it was designed for the IBM-3270 terminals, it is now usually used via terminal emulation (e.g., RUMBA) on PCs.

Messages are typically in IBM's EBCDIC format rather than ASCII. When a user creates and sends a message, it can be delivered directly to a reader queue to be fetched by the recipient. Or, if the recipient is not local, it may be routed to another PROFS system using RSCS, the remote spooling and communications subsystem.

Although there is no X.500-like directory support, there is a systemwide nickname file called OFSUAD, which simplifies the entry of foreign addresses. In contrast to X.500, however, it must be kept up-to-date manually.

Verimation MEMO

MEMO is another mail application built for the IBM mainframe. It offers a significant amount of connectivity, with gateways to PROFS, SNADS, X.400 and SMTP, and is used by millions of users worldwide. However, like PROFS, it was built for terminals and does not take advantage of the new world of PCs. The trend, therefore, is for migration to some of the newer products.

Gateways

As we have seen in the few backbones we have looked at, there are a number of different ways in which messaging systems can vary. Nevertheless, they accomplish the same function. It is the job of the gateway to convert from one implementation to another. This process can be broken down into two separate areas:

1. **Message connectivity**: Making sure messages from one backbone arrive intact to the other backbone;
2. **Directory synchronization**: Ensuring that users from one mail system are able to look up in their own directory users from the other mail system.

In some cases, the gateway has the additional task of having one network protocol running on one side and another on the other side. It then has to convert the data for the appropriate protocol. The machine itself may also be used to convert data from other applications.

Message connectivity will involve:

1. Receiving each message;
2. Converting the message format and address to that of the new system;
3. Routing the message on its way.

Directory synchronization is accomplished by:

1. Exporting a source directory;
2. Adapting the addresses to a syntax that can be understood by the destination;
3. Importing the directory at the destination.

Message Router Gateway

You can see a schematic representation of a message router gateway in Figure 8-4. Basically, all it does is tie together a message router (MAILbus) backbone with an X.400 (MAILbus 400) backbone. To do this it needs to be known to both networks as a gateway so that it can relay messages between them. While forwarding the messages, it performs two important tasks that we see, in one form or another, in all of the gateways:

1. Address resolution;
2. Content conversion.

We have already seen that Message Router uses an entirely different addressing mechanism than does X.400. If we want to send messages from one backbone to the other, we obviously need to have some way of mapping the addresses from one format to the other. We can do this either exhaustively by entering the mapping for each message router user in the X.500 tree, or we can use a partial address mapping to map the external domain message router to a particular branch in our X.400 addressing scheme.

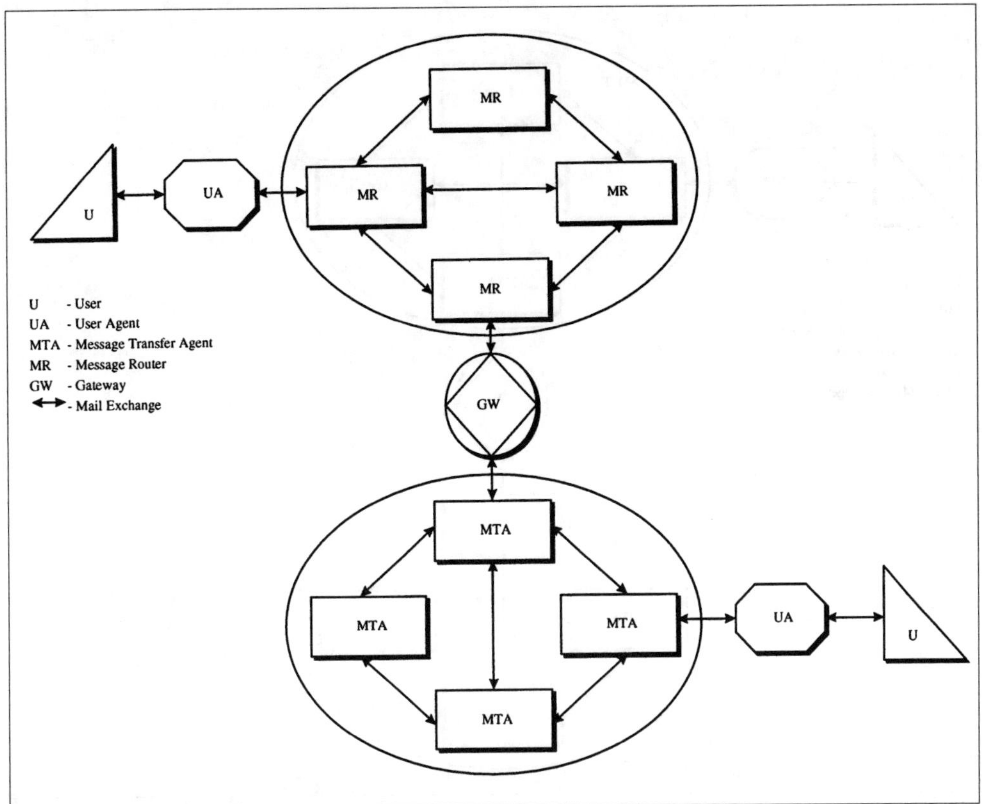

Figure 8-4. *Message Router Gateway*

The other task is to convert the messages between the X.400 format and Message Router's so-called NBS (National Bureau of Standards) format. It needs to preserve as many of the attributes as it can (note that Message Router only supports the 1984 X.400 fields) and ensure that all of the bodyparts are tagged correctly for the respective backbones.

SMTP Gateway

In Figure 8-5 you see the same diagram for SMTP as you saw for Message Router. There is no major difference in the schematic, since they have essentially the same structure.

Much of what was said for the Message Router gateway could also be said for the SMTP gateway. Again we need to convert the

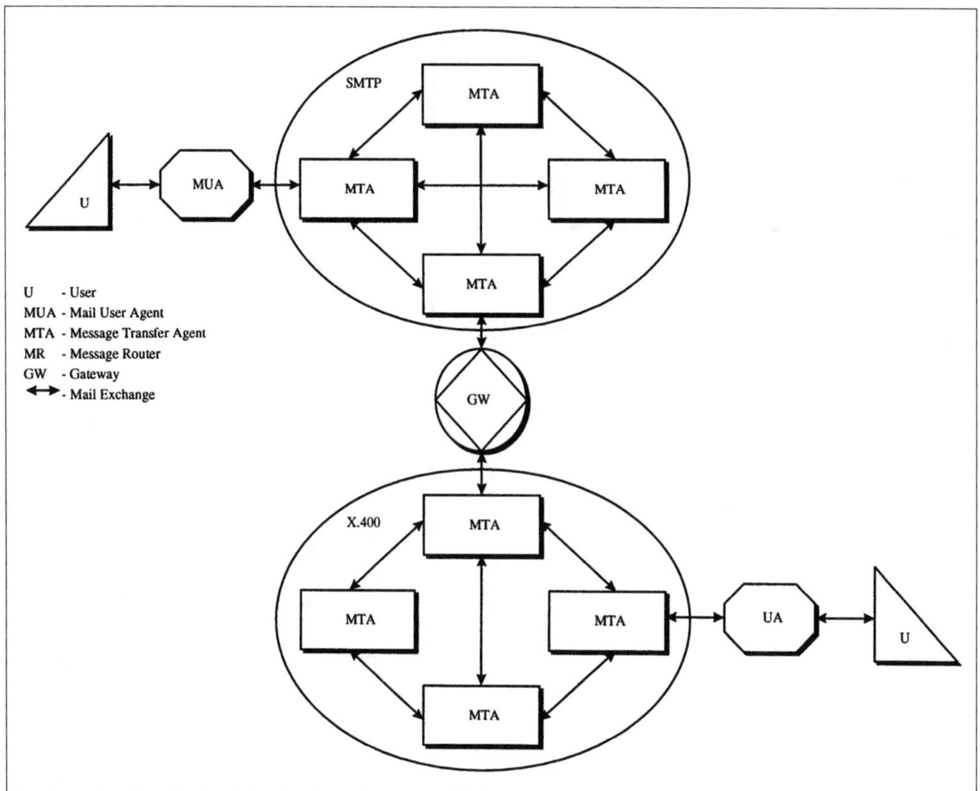

Figure 8-5. *SMTP Gateway*

addressing from a style of "`John.Rhoton(aui.mts.dec.com`" to "`C=AT;A=ADA;P=Digital;O=Digital;OU=AUI;CN=John Rhoton`."

As always, we have the three options of an exhaustive per-user mapping, partial address mapping and domain defined attributes (DDAs). While we could use whatever mechanism we like to embed the SMTP address in an X.400 address, and vice versa, a proprietary scheme would not work very well in a heterogeneous network with several different mail applications on each backbone.

To solve this problem, RFC 1327 has defined a standard. It addresses the issues of interoperability between the two backbones by focusing on the analogies and creating a mapping between them. And, as part of the task of interoperating, it dictates the syntax of embedded addresses.

When it comes to converting the content, we have more significant differences than for Message Router. The attributes are not as closely aligned, and the message structure is much different. In particular, we have the problem that SMTP expects seven-bit ASCII documents. Since most Internet mail applications now support MIME, the SMTP gateway does too. It converts between MIME and the X.400 format when exchanging mail between the two networks.

Telematic Gateways

Not everyone in the world has an e-mail account. Many people can still be reached only via fax and telex. But that does not mean our users should need to type telex messages or feed faxes in by hand. We can let them send messages in the same way regardless of the recipient's equipment.

To do this, we need to have a gateway that connects our X.400 network with a fax modem or a telex terminal (see Figure 8-6). If the users specify the addresses correctly, we can convert them to fax and telex numbers and the messages will go on to the intended recipients.

One telematic gateway that is very popular in Austria is MBTOPCALL, which connects MAILbus 400 to a TOPCALL box that can send and receive faxes. There are other gateways you can find to best suit your needs. In some cases the administrative domains provide gateways that you can use for a price so that you do not need to bother with installing the hardware and software of a dedicated gateway.

The two main issues with telematic gateways are the addressing and the formatting. You have already seen that we usually indicate an X.400 address with a format similar to:

```
C=AT; A=ADA; P=Digital; O=Digital; OU=AUI; CN=John Rhoton;
```

This does not work particularly well with a fax, which expects a telephone number and doesn't really care what the recipient's name is. Some creative minds could no doubt find a way to put a number into one of the fields, but we don't need a work-around, because the ITU

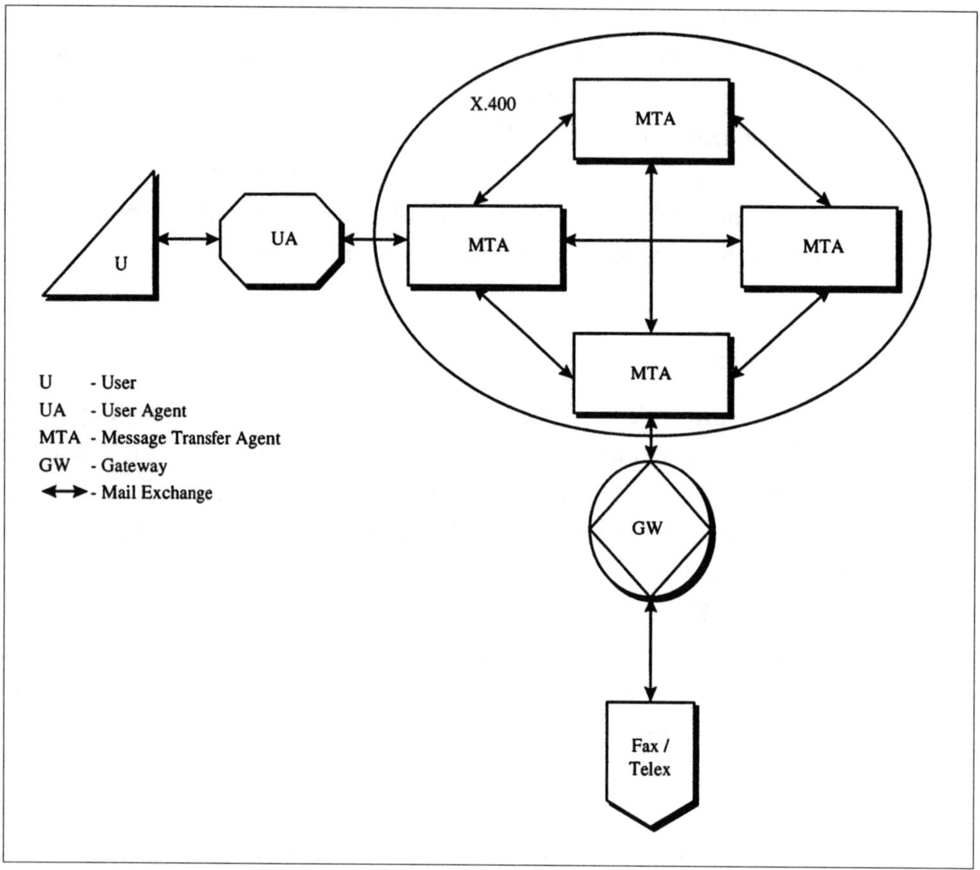

Figure 8-6. *Telematic Gateways*

foresaw this need in its specification. They created another field, called X121. You can enter an address of the format of

```
C=AT; A=ADA; P=TOPCALL; X121=866303199
```

which is much more elegant. So far, so good. You can send a message to the X121 address, and the text of the message will appear on the fax machine. If this is the recipient's private fax machine, there should be no confusion as to whose fax it is. But this will not often be the case. A number of users will share the same machine, and you will need to identify the recipient in the text of the fax.

You could name the addressee in the text, but that would cause confusion if you wanted to send the same message to multiple recipients.

What you need is some way for the person to be identified in the address and for the gateway to place the name in the formatted output.

The best way is to put the names and other organizational information in the normal fields:

```
C=AT; A=ADA; P=TOPCALL; X121=866303199; OU=AUI; CN=John Rhoton;
```

and let the gateway take care of the rest. MBTOPCALL provides a means of specifying a template file with the gateway or with the individual fax using a DDA. In the template, we can indicate where the fields should go and how they should look.

The other consideration for all gateways, but particularly acute for a telematic gateway, is conversion. A telex box will not be able to read a graphic or any PC document. We need to make sure that the permissible types are defined and other bodyparts are either converted or returned to the sender.

Other Gateways

Every messaging environment is an opportunity for a connection. The only other MAILbus 400 gateway currently in operation is the SNADS gateway to connect to SNADS/DIA-based products, including IBM Office Vision/400, IBM Office Vision/MVS with IBM DISOSS, and Verimation MEMO.

Other companies, like ISOCOR, offer interconnection to LAN-based e-mail packages, like Lotus Notes, cc:Mail or Microsoft Mail.

Highlights

- The various backbones offer much the same set of functionality but vastly different implementations. Some of the features include:

  Network requirements;
  Backbone topology;
  Addressing syntax;
  Structure of messages;
  Directory support.

- Connection of two dissimilar mail systems involves addressing:

  Network connectivity;
  Mail connectivity, including address mapping and content conversion;
  Directory support.

References

MAILbus 400: Getting Started	AA-QSGHB-TE
MAILbus 400: Message Router Gateway for OpenVMS VAX Managing	AA-Q8QRC-TE
MAILbus 400: Message Transfer Agent Planning and Setup	AA-Q89MC-TE
MAILbus 400: Message Transfer Agent Tuning and Problem Solving	AA-Q89NC-TE

Alvestrand, H. 1993. *Equivalences between 1988 X.400 and RFC-822 Message Bodies* (RFC 1494).

Alvestrand, H., et al. 1993. *Mapping between X.400 and RFC-822 Message Bodies* (RFC 1495).

Hardcastle-Kille, S. 1992. *Mapping between X.400(1988) / ISO 10021 and RFC 822* (RFC 1327).

Redmond, Tony. 1997. *Microsoft Exchange Server V5.0: Planning Design and Implementation.* Boston: Digital Press. ISBN 1-55558-189-7.

Chapter 9

Summing It Up

Similarities Between X.400 and SMTP

While X.400 and SMTP differ in many ways, it is important to realize that they perform the same function. That function is to route mail from one mail system to another through a wide area network. In order to do this, they employ different approaches, but the requirements laid on them are the same. As a result, there are many similarities between the two protocols.

Table 9-1 shows some analogies between X.400/OSI and SMTP/IP.

Table 9-1. *Analogies Between X.400/OSI and SMTP/IP*

X.400/OSI	SMTP/IP
CONS: Connection-oriented network service	TCP
CLNS: Connectionless network service	UDP
NSAP	IP address
TSEL	IP protocol number (TCP or UDP)
SSEL/PSEL	Socket
PSAP	Port
P2/P22	RFC 822 + RFCs 2045–2049 MIME
P1	RFC 821 — SMTP
P7	POP3 / IMAP4
X.500	DNS
DAP	LDAP

In Favor of X.400

As we have seen, the designers at the CCITT/ITU and ISO were very fond of designing elegant architectures. They introduced structure to the design of networks and mail systems, which helped clarify the discussion of functionality and protocols.

From them we have the OSI network model and a clear definition of the components in a mail system or directory. They also designed a comprehensive mail and directory architecture, much of which has also found its way into the Internet's mail paradigm.

In addition to the architectural specification, X.400 still has a few technical advantages over SMTP:

- X.400 offers a succinct message format.
- X.400 can restrict the topology of the message backbone.
- X.400 offers better notifications.
- X.400 is closely affiliated with X.435, the current standard for EDI.
- X.400 is more closely tied to X.500, which offers a more comprehensive directory than LDAP.

In Favor of SMTP

The Internet has not been as concerned with architecture. Instead, it has opted for responding quickly to needs and to providing guidelines that are simple to implement and have been shown to work. This approach means that it has been easy for software developers to incorporate Internet standards, and these standards now have the momentum of the market behind them.

- SMTP is simple to implement and maintain.
- SMTP has the momentum of the Internet behind it.
- SMTP is flexible and adaptable; new functionality is made available more quickly.

The practical result of this is that new functionality and specification are appearing on the Internet at a very fast pace.

SMTP's technical advantages over X.400 are not yet overwhelming:

- Improved facilities for specifying encryption;
- Better support for message stores with IMAP.

But it will not be long before the functionality of the Internet unambiguously surpasses that of X.400.

The Verdict

Describing technology is very much like shooting at a moving target: Anytime we write something, the information is surpassed by the time you read it. E-mail is not excluded from this, and it has been both exciting and intimidating to watch it evolve as I have written.

At present it looks very much like the Internet is dictating the e-mail standards. Since they have authored, and therefore embrace, SMTP as the primary messaging backbone, there is very little doubt that the next few years will see SMTP outpace X.400.

This does not means that X.400 is likely to disappear soon. SMTP still has a way to go before it has unambiguously outclassed X.400. And even when this happens, many companies will prefer to keep X.400. They may have applications that require it, or they may simply not wish to expend the effort to migrate from one backbone to another. Further complicating the matter are a number of trends in the marketplace, such as:

- Interest in electronic commerce;
- Mobile computing;
- Security requirements, including encryption and certification;
- Web-based access for use and administration.

It is difficult to say how these developments will affect the choice of backbones, or even whether they will impact the very existence of mail backbones in years to come.

The Next Step

That completes our brief journey into the world of electronic mail and directories. I hope you enjoyed it and are interested in finding out more about the standards and the products. If so, you will soon discover that there is a lot more to know than we have covered here and you will never be in danger of knowing it all.

X.400

The best way to learn is by doing, and if you have access to the products you may want to verify everything I have said. One of the fastest ways to get up to speed is to attend training seminars. Digital offers regular courses on MAILbus 400 and X.500 that will teach you how to design and manage an X.400 configuration.

If you are keen on learning on your own and are using MAILbus 400, there is a guide called *MAILbus 400: Getting Started,* which will have you on your way in no time. It assumes very little knowledge of X.400 and shows you how to set up a simple environment. Once you have that working, you can take a look at *MAILbus 400: Message Transfer Agent Planning and Setup,* to see how you can extend the functionality to a larger environment and take care of your specific requirements. That should take care of you for a while, but at some point you will have a functional environment and will need to track down the occasional problem or fine-tune your configuration. That is where *MAILbus 400: Message Transfer Agent Tuning and Problem Solving* comes in. You may also want to connect the odd gateway, and will find documentation on them, too. I have referenced the MAILbus 400 documentation extensively and can commend its clear and thorough explanations of a complex set of topics.

There are a number of companies besides Digital that specialize in mail products such as ISOCOR and PMDF. They also offer a wide range of products, and you can gain further insight into mail by reading their documentation or browsing their Web sites.

Maybe you are interested in the standards themselves. Most people try to stay away from them, but you might want to write code that is compatible with them, or you might need to troubleshoot a problem that requires getting down to the nuts and bolts. You can, of course, order the standards themselves, and at some level of technical detail you might have to. I will warn you that the standards are rather terse and advise you to reference an accompanying text until you feel comfortable with them. One book to help you with the X.400 standard is *Electronic Mail* by Sara Radicati (1992).

Ultimately, to fully understand electronic mailing, you need a good understanding of networking. There are many books on the subject, but I am sure you will not find a more widely accepted treatment than Andrew Tanenbaum's in *Computer Networks*, now in its third edition. The book has been the standard text in many, if not most, universities. I should point out that for a discussion of OSI networking, you will find more information in the first two editions. But if you want to keep up with the current trends, you will greatly appreciate the major changes in the third.

If you are a loyal Digital customer and have a DECnet network in place, you should consider *DECnet Phase V: An OSI Implementation*, by James Martin and Joe Leben. If you are equipped with a reasonable understanding of the OSI model before you read it, you will find it a clear and well-written description of how Digital has implemented the OSI protocols.

SMTP

For SMTP, the most authoritative sources of information are the RFCs themselves. I have mentioned the most important mail-related standards in this book, and they are as good a place as any to start. They will give you a more in-depth understanding of

Internet mail. Some of these are quite easy to read, while others are longer and more complex. If you find any of them overly difficult, you can try looking at their (now obsolete) predecessors. A look at an original specification can often be enlightening. There are also some books on networking and the Internet protocols, which may help you further.

References

MAILbus 400:Getting Started AA-QSGHB-TE

MAILbus 400: Message Transfer Agent Planning and Setup AA-Q89MC-TE

MAILbus 400: Message Transfer Agent Tuning and Problem Solving AA-Q89NC-TE

MAILbus 400: Message Router Gateway for OpenVMS VAX Managing AA-Q8QRC-TE

MAILbus 400: Message Store Managing AA-Q75BC-TE

Digital X.500 Directory Service Management AA-QEVEC-TE

DECnet/OSI for OpenVMS Introduction and User's Guide AA-Q191E-TE

DECnet/OSI Network Management AA-Q18UE-TE

DECnet/OSI Planning Guide AA-QBTHD-TE

DECnet/OSI Problem Solving AA-Q18ZD-TE

Martin, James, and Joe Leben. 1992. *DECnet Phase V: An OSI Implementation*. Boston: Digital Press.

Radicati, S. 1992. *Electronic Mail: An Introduction to the X.400 Message Handling Standards*. New York: McGraw-Hill. ISBN 0-07-051104-7.

Tanenbaum, Andrew S. 1996. *Computer Networks*. Englewood Cliffs, N.J.: Prentice Hall.

Information on the World Wide Web

General Web Resources

E-mail Web resources:

```
http://andrew2.andrew.cmu.edu/cyrus/email/
```

The canonical Internet *versus* X.400 debate:

```
http://domen.uninett.no/~hta/x400/debate/
```

Mail-related FAQs:

```
http://www.cs.ruu.nl/wais/html/na-dir/mail/.html
```

FAQ for the mailing list MHSNEWS/newsgroup comp.protocols.iso.X400:

```
http://domen.uninett.no/~hta/x400/faq-mhsnews.html (html format)
ftp://aun.uninett.no/pub/mail/x400faq/FAQ-mhsnews.text (text format)
```

Index to X.400 Web pages:

```
http://domen.uninett.no/~hta/x400/index.html
```

X.400 on the Web:

```
http://www.to.icl.fi/~jhe/x400/index.html
```

Standards

RFC repository:

```
ftp://ds.internic.net/rfc/
```

List of ITU–T recommendations:

```
http://www.itu.ch/publications/itu-t/itut.htm
```

The X.400 standards:

```
http://domen.uninett.no/~hta/x400/standards.html
```

Products and Services

Hotmail:

`http://www.hotmail.com/`

Rocketmail:

`http://www.rocketmail.com/`

Innosoft Internation, Inc.:

`http://www.innosoft.com/`

S/MIME:

`http://www.rsa.com/rsa/S-MIME/`

ISOCOR:

`http://www.isocor.com/`

Microsoft Exchange:

`http://www.microsoft.com/exchange`

Lotus:

`http://www.lotus.com/`

Appendix A

OSI Implementation

Since some of my examples in this book use MAILbus 400 and Digital X.500, both of which rely on DECnet/OSI, it is worth making a few comments about DECnet. It is an implementation of the OSI model, and as such, will give you an idea of what the theory can look like in practice.

Keep in mind the following points, however: First, the OSI model is not very detailed. As a result, while there is a core of common protocols, not everyone implements everything that is optional.

Digital also has the responsibility of maintaining backward compatibility with its previous version of DECnet (Phase IV), which was not OSI compliant. So it has added modules that make Phase IV requests continue to work in a Phase V network. You would not find these anywhere else.

The OSI model does not define how the management of the network needs to be implemented. DECnet has something called NCL. This too is Digital-specific, although you should find equivalent functionality in any OSI network.

In Figure A-1, you can see how a typical DECnet OSI node can have multiple stacks running concurrently. On the left you see what is largely a CLNS stack running across an ethernet or FDDI cable. On the right you see a CONS (X.25) stack.

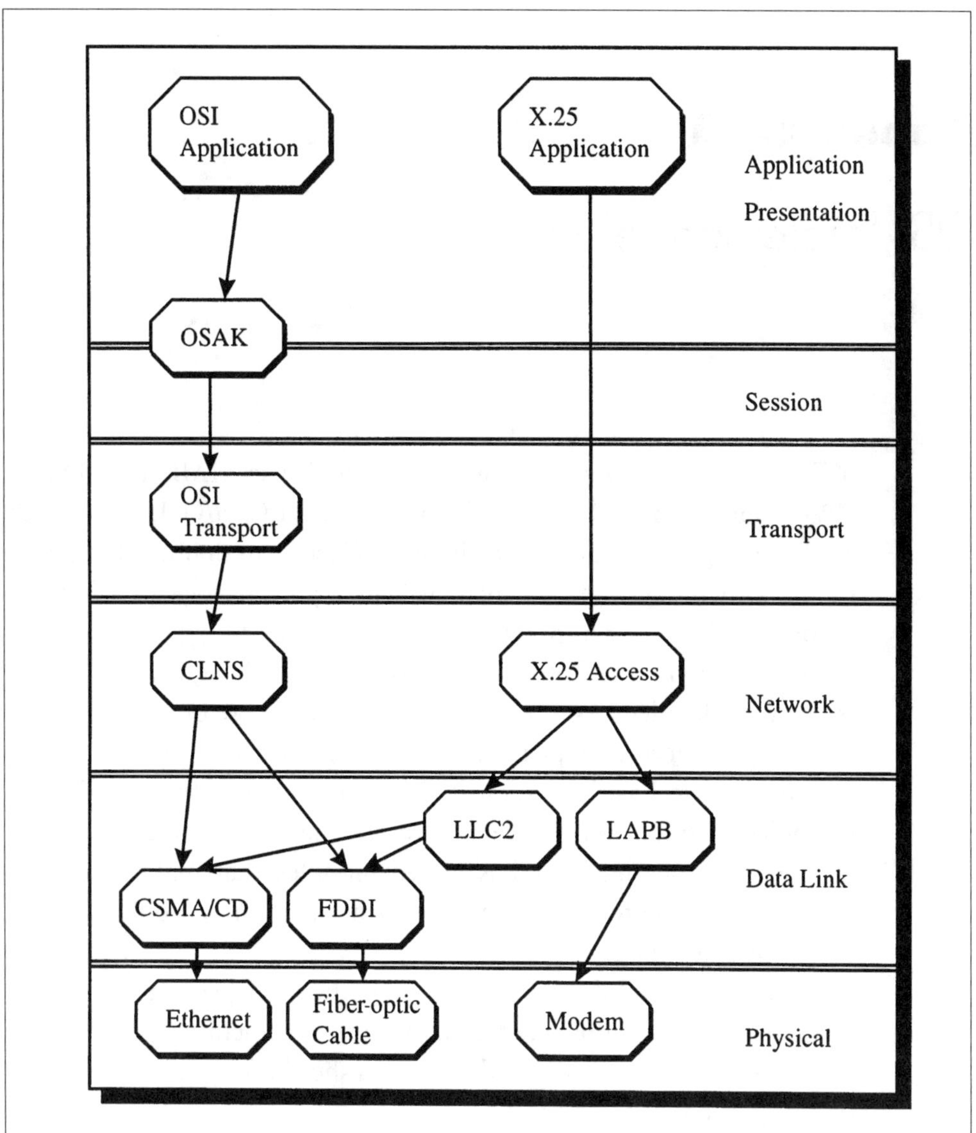

Figure A-1. *Some of DECnet's Protocols*

Appendix B

X.400 Example

```
CONTEXT 0
  <Message>
  SET
    <TransferEnvelope>
    MTS_ID
      <MTS Identifier>
      GDI
        COUNTRY
          PRINTABLE            Len 2
            "GB" Hex 47 42
        ADMD
          PRINTABLE            Len 1
            " " Hex 20
        PRINTABLE              Len 12
          "BBS NIRELAND"
      IA5                      Len 24
        <LocalId>
        "7FD072C011D059BF00080280"
    ORNAME
      <Originator>
      SEQ
        <StandardAttributes>
        COUNTRY
          PRINTABLE            Len 2
            "GB" Hex 47 42
        ADMD
          PRINTABLE            Len 1
            " " Hex 20
        CONTEXT 2
          <PrivateDomainName>
          PRINTABLE            Len 12
            "BBS NIRELAND"
        CONTEXT 3              Len 38
```

```
        <OrganizationalName>
        "BBS DIRECTORATE OF INFORMATION SYSTEMS"
      CONTEXT 5
        <PersonalName>
        CONTEXT 0             Len 8
          <surname>
          "McCarthy"
        CONTEXT 1             Len 4
          <given-name>
          "Mark" Hex 4d 61 72 6b
      CONTEXT 6
        <OrganizationalUnitNames>
        PRINTABLE             Len 13
          "MESSAGE STORE"
    SET
      <ORname Extensions>
      SEQ
        CONTEXT 0             Len 1
          Hex 1 Dec 1
        CONTEXT 1
          <CommonName (Printable)>
          PRINTABLE           Len 13
            "MARK MCCARTHY"
  EITS
    <EITs>
    CONTEXT 0                 Len 2
      <BuiltinEits>
      " " Hex 20
  BUILTIN                     Len 1
    <ContentType (built-in)>
    Hex 16 Dec 22
  CONT_ID                     Len 12
    <ContentIdentifier>
    "test message"
  PRIORITY                    Len 1
    <Priority>
    Hex 2 Dec 2
  MSG_IND                     Len 2
    <MessageIndicators>
    "0" Hex 30
  CONTEXT 2
    <Recipients>
    SET
      ORNAME
        SEQ
          <StandardAttributes>
          COUNTRY
            PRINTABLE         Len 2
              "gb" Hex 67 62
          ADMD
```

```
          PRINTABLE              Len 1
            " " Hex 20
        CONTEXT 2
          <PrivateDomainName>
          PRINTABLE              Len 12
            "bbs nireland"
        CONTEXT 3                Len 12
          <OrganizationalName>
          "bbs exchange"
        CONTEXT 5
          <PersonalName>
          CONTEXT 0              Len 6
            <surname>
            "rhoton"
          CONTEXT 1              Len 4
            <given-name>
            "john" Hex 6a 6f 68 6e
    CONTEXT 0                    Len 1
      <OriginallySpecifiedRecipientNo>
      Hex 1 Dec 1
    CONTEXT 1                    Len 2
      <PerRecipientIndicators>
      Hex d0
    CONTEXT 3
      <Extensions>
      SEQ
        CONTEXT 0                Len 1
          <Extension>
          Hex 6 Dec 6
        <RequestedDeliveryMethod>
        CONTEXT 1                Len 2
          <Criticality>
          Hex 00
        CONTEXT 2
          SEQ
            INTEGER              Len 1
              Hex 0 Dec 0
OCTETSTRING            Len 425
  <Content>
  Hex a0 82 01 a5 31 82 01 84 6b 81 a1 60 81 80 30 66
      61 04 13 02 47 42 62 03 13 01 20 a2 0e 13 0c 4e
      48 53 20 4e 49 52 45 4c 41 4e 44 83 26 4e 48 53
      20 44 49 52 45 43 54 4f 52 41 54 45 20 4f 46 20
      49 4e 46 4f 52 4d 41 54 49 4f 4e 20 53 59 53 54
      45 4d 53 a5 10 80 08 4d 63 4b 69 6c 6c 6f 70 81
      04 4d 61 72 6b a6 0f 13 0d 4d 45 53 53 41 47 45
      20 53 54 4f 52 45 31 16 30 14 80 01 01 a1 0f 13
      0d 4d 41 52 4b 20 4d 43 4b 49 4c 4c 4f 50 13 1c
      47 55 49 44 3a 51 41 55 6c 6d 57 37 39 5a 30 42
      47 36 58 41 41 67 72 38 39 4a 67 67 a0 81 83 60
```

```
81 80 30 66 61 04 13 02 47 42 62 03 13 01 20 a2
0e 13 0c 4e 48 53 20 4e 49 52 45 4c 41 4e 44 83
26 4e 48 53 20 44 49 52 45 43 54 4f 52 41 54 45
20 4f 46 20 49 4e 46 4f 52 4d 41 54 49 4f 4e 20
53 59 53 54 45 4d 53 a5 10 80 08 4d 63 4b 69 6c
6c 6f 70 81 04 4d 61 72 6b a6 0f 13 0d 4d 45 53
53 41 47 45 20 53 54 4f 52 45 31 16 30 14 80 01
01 a1 0f 13 0d 4d 41 52 4b 20 4d 43 4b 49 4c 4c
4f 50 a2 45 31 43 a0 3d 60 3b 30 39 61 04 13 02
67 62 62 03 13 01 20 a2 0e 13 0c 6e 68 73 20 6e
69 72 65 6c 61 6e 64 83 0c 6e 68 73 20 65 78 63
68 61 6e 67 65 a5 0e 80 06 72 68 6f 74 6f 6e 81
04 6a 6f 68 6e 81 02 05 c0 a8 0e 14 0c 74 65 73
74 20 6d 65 73 73 61 67 65 8c 01 02 30 1b a0 19
31 00 16 15 54 65 73 74 20 6d 65 73 73 61 67 65
20 76 69 61 20 72 75 61 00
```

Appendix C

MIME Example

```
From: John Rhoton <John.Rhoton@dbo-exchangeist.dbo.dec.com>
To: "'106107.3054@compuserve.com'" <106107.3054@compuserve.com>
Subject: Two Binary attachments
Date: Sat, 11 Jan 1997 15:24:28 -0000
X-Mailer:  Microsoft Exchange Server Internet Mail Connector Version 4.0.994.63
Mime-Version: 1.0
Content-Type: multipart/mixed; boundary="---- =_NextPart_000_01BBFFD3.8ACB9240"

This message is in MIME format. Since your mail reader does not understand
this format, some or all of this message may not be legible.

------ =_NextPart_000_01BBFFD3.8ACB9240
Content-Type: text/plain; charset="us-ascii"
Content-Transfer-Encoding: 7bit

This message contains a Microsoft Word Document and a Microsoft
Excel Spreadsheet

=================================================================
John Rhoton -- Messaging Consultant - Digital Equipment Corporation
=================================================================
Wisma Digital                          Digital Equipment Ireland
4, Jalan Bersatu 13/4,                 Park House
46200 Petaling Jaya,                   North Circular Road
Selangor Darul Ehsan.                  Dublin
Malaysia                               Ireland
=================================================================
John.Rhoton@msa.mts.dec.com            John.Rhoton@dbo.mts.dec.com
=================================================================

------ =_NextPart_000_01BBFFD3.8ACB9240
Content-Type: application/msword; name="x.doc"
Content-Transfer-Encoding: base64
```

0M8R4KGxGuEAAAAAAAAAAAAAAAAAAAAAPgADAP7/CQAGAAAAAAAAAAAAAAABAAAAIQAAAAAAAAAAAA
EAAAIwAAAAEAAAD+////AAAAACAAAAD///
... (many lines of 80 characters)
AAAAAAAAAAAAAAAAAAAAAAAAAAAAAAAAAAAAAAAAAAAAAAAAAAAAAAAAAAAAAAAAAAAAAAAAAAAA
AAAAAAAAAAAAAAAAAAAAAAAAAAAAAAAAAAAAAAAAAAAAAAAAAAAAAAAAAAAAAAAAAAAAAAAAAAAA
AAAAAAAAAAAAAAAAAAAAAAAAAAAAAAAAAAAAAAAAAAAAAAAAAAAAAAAAAAAAAAAAAAAAAAAAAAAA
AAAAAAAAAAAAAAAAAAAAAAAAAA==

```
------ =_NextPart_000_01BBFFD3.8ACB9240
Content-Type: application/octet-stream; name="y.xls"
Content-Transfer-Encoding: base64
```

0M8R4KGxGuEAAAAAAAAAAAAAAAAAAAAAPgADAP7/CQAGAAAAAAAAAAAAAAABAAAAGQAAAAAAAAAAAA
EAAA/v///wAAAAD+////AAAAABgAAAD///
... (many lines of 80 characters)
AAAAAAAAAAAAKAACAQEAAAADAAAA/////wAAAAAAAAAAAAAAAAAAAAAAAAAAAAAAAAAAAAAAAAAA
AAAAAAgAAAAAEAAAAAAAAAAUARABvAGMAdQBtAGUAbgB0AFMAdQBtAG0AYQByAHkASQBuAGYAbwBy
AG0AYQB0AGkAbwBuAAAAPABAAKQiQAA4AAIB////////////////AAAAAGQ6QAAAAAAAAAAAAAAA
AAAAAAAAAAAAAAAAAAAAAAAAEAAAAAAQAAACAAAA

```
------ =_NextPart_000_01BBFFD3.8ACB9240-
```

Appendix D

POP3 Example

```
MSAM03» telnet 16.157.64.25 110
Trying...16.157.64.25
Connected to 16.157.64.25.
Escape character is '^]'.

+OK Der Microsoft Exchange POP3-Server (Version 5.0.1389.6) ist betriebsbereit.

USER rhoton

+OK

PASS badpassword

-ERR Logon failure: unknown user name or bad password.

user rhoton

+OK

pass goodpassword

+OK Der Benutzer wurde erfolgreich angemeldet.

stat

+OK 3 3154

list

+OK
```

```
1 676
2 1526
3 952
.

retr 1


+OK
Received: from pobox1.pa.dec.com by mcpserver.msa.dec.com with SMTP (Microsoft
Exchange Internet Mail Service Ver
sion 5.0.1389.3)
        id FXVSF3ZF; Fri, 28 Feb 1997 22:38:13 +0800
Received: by pobox1.pa.dec.com; id AA21112; Fri, 28 Feb 97 06:39:35 -0800
Received: by dubdtp.dbo.dec.com (5.57/Ultrix3.0-C)
        id AA10518; Fri, 28 Feb 97 14:45:09 GMT
Received: by dbo-excha
ngeist.dublin.dbo.dec.com with Internet Mail Service (5.0.1389.3)
        id <01BC2585.97663FF0@dbo-exchangeist.dublin.dbo.dec.com>; Fri, 28 Feb
 1997 14:42:16 -0000
Message-Id: <E081F44FDB37D011A5480020AFF54A231E3CD6@dbo-
exchangeist.dublin.dbo.dec.com>
From: "
John Rhoton (Dublin)" <John.Rhoton@dbo-exchangeist.dbo.dec.com>
To: John.Rhoton@mcpserver.msa.dec.com
Subject: FW: Visits to Japan and T
hailand
Date: Fri, 28 Feb 1997 14:40:59 -0000
X-Priority: 3
Mime-Version: 1.0
X-Mailer: Internet Mail Service (5.0.1389.3)
Content-Type: text/plain




> ----------
> From:               Tony Redmond
> Sent:               28 February 1997 14:40:59
> To:   John Rhoton (Dublin)
> Subject:            RE: Visits to Japan and Thailand
> Auto forwarded by a Rule
>
Ah!  But will YOU still be there
?

> -----Original Message-----
> From: John Rhoton (Dublin)
> Sent: 28 February 1997 08:09
> To:   'Tony Redmond'
> Subject:            RE: Vis
its to Japan and Thailand
>
```

```
>
>       Sounds good.  Let me know if you are in the area.
>
>       John
>
> [Tony Redmond]
.

quit


+OK Die Verbindung mit dem Microsoft Exchange POP3-Server (Version 5.0.1389.6)
wird getrennt.


Remote connection closed
```

Appendix E

SMTP Header

```
Received: from rg71rw.reo.dec.com by dbo-exchangeist.dbo.dec.com with SMTP
(Microsoft Exchange Internet Mail Connector Version 4.0.994.63)
     id B10YCBGY; Wed, 15 Jan 1997 00:42:42 -0000
Received: from mts.dec.com by rg71rw.reo.dec.com (PMDF V5.0-7 #15552)
 id <01IE7L8HERSG91WGGL@rg71rw.reo.dec.com> for
 JohnR@dbo-exchangeist.dbo.dec.com; Wed, 15 Jan 1997 00:25:30 +0000 (GMT)
Received: from mail.vbo.dec.com (mail.vbo.dec.com)
 by valmts.vbe.dec.com (PMDF V5.0-7 #16475)
 id <01IE7RVOSE0G00GLNV@valmts.vbe.dec.com> for John.Rhoton@dbo.mts.dec.com;
 Tue, 14 Jan 1997 20:11:43 +0100 (CET)
Received: from server21.digital.fr (server21.digital.fr [193.56.15.21])
 by mail.vbo.dec.com (8.7.3/8.7) with ESMTP id UAA05316 for
 <John.Rhoton@dbo.mts.dec.com>; Tue, 14 Jan 1997 20:11:15 +0100 (MET)
Received: from hil-img-2.compuserve.com
 (hil-img-2.compuserve.com [149.174.177.132])
 by server21.digital.fr (8.7.5/8.7) with SMTP id UAA25548 for
 <John.Rhoton@dbo.mts.dec.com>; Tue, 14 Jan 1997 20:12:49 +0100 (MET)
Received: by hil-img-2.compuserve.com (8.6.10/5.950515) id OAA03332; Tue,
 14 Jan 1997 14:06:21 -0500
Received: with PMDF-MR; Tue, 14 Jan 1997 20:17:24 +0000 (GMT)
MR-Received: by mta DUB01; Relayed; Tue, 14 Jan 1997 20:19:33 +0000
MR-Received: by mta RDGMTS; Relayed; Tue, 14 Jan 1997 20:17:47 +0000
Date: Tue, 14 Jan 1997 19:05:53 +0000 (GMT)
From: John Rhoton <106107.3054@compuserve.com>
Subject: Ist wieder auf dem Weg gelegen !
To: JR <John.Rhoton@dbo.mts.dec.com>
Message-id: <199701141406_MC1-E7D-5429@compuserve.com>
Autoforwarded: false
MIME-version: 1.0
Content-type: TEXT/PLAIN; CHARSET=ISO-8859-1
Content-transfer-encoding: QUOTED-PRINTABLE
Priority: non-urgent
X400-MTS-identifier: [;42710241107991/5512012@VALMTS]
Hop-count: 5
```

Appendix F
MAILbus 400 Architecture

Overview

NCL/EMA

Every network needs a means of managing it. DECnet employs an architecture called EMA (enterprise management architecture) which is depicted in Figure F-1. All of the related entities that can be

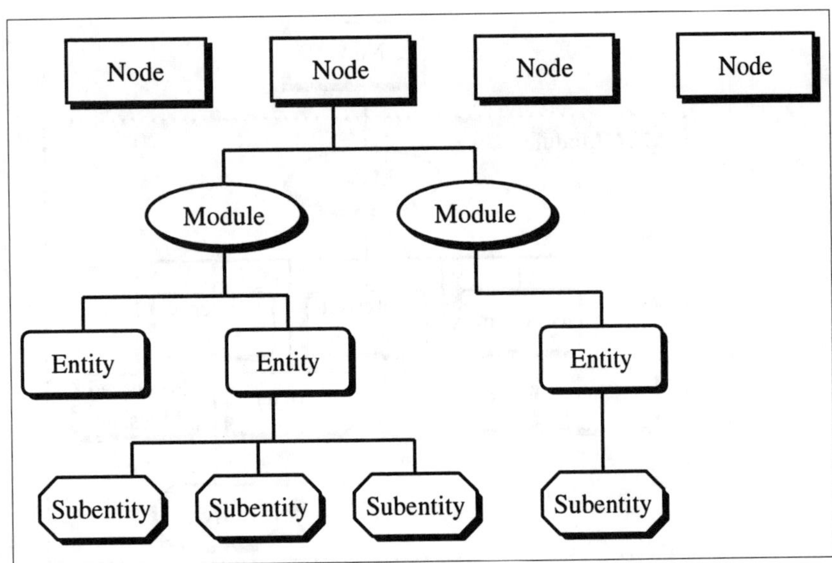

Figure F-1. *Entity Naming Hierarchy*

managed are grouped together into modules. Examples of modules are a DSA module for X.500 and MTA and MTS modules for MAILbus 400. In some cases the entities are too complex to be represented singly. The architecture allows the entity to spawn off subentities, which can be managed separately. To manage the actual entities you need to use an application called a director. The standard director for DECnet is called NCL.

MTA Entity

As we have already seen, message transfer agents are responsible for routing MPDUs within a message transport system. They will be configured differently with every implementation of X.400, and every application will have its own way of accessing and representing the data they access.

Nevertheless, they all perform the same tasks and have essentially the same objects with which to work. Figure F-2 shows these objects

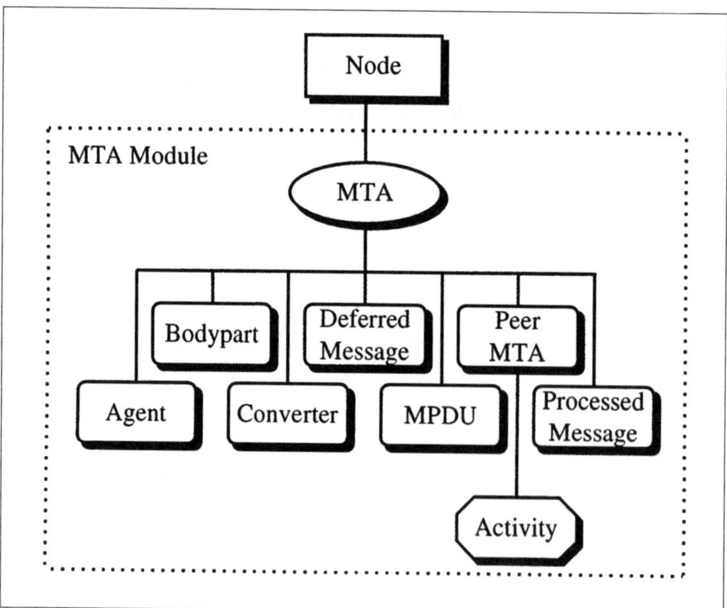

Figure F-2. *MTA Entity*

in terms of MAILbus 400, where they are managed using an EMA director and are called entities. A quick look at these entities should give you an idea of what the MTA does and how it does it.

- **Agent:** A user agent, message store or gateway. You can manage and examine certain characteristics, such as how to invoke them, the type of interface they use to communicate with the MTA (e.g., XAPI), whether to archive incoming and outgoing messages, and statistical information (e.g., number of MPDUs).
- **Bodypart:** A bodypart format recognized by the MTA. Every document type (e.g., ODIF, Word, ASCII, WPS-PLUS) must be registered in order for the MTA to know what it is and perform appropriate conversions. A bodypart can have a mnemonic name, but it must also be identified by an encoded information type (EIT), which is a set of universally agreed-upon tags for all the file types in circulation.

  That is the theory. In practice, not all formats have an EIT, and some may have more than one if different vendors assigned different values. Still, if you know what EITs are entering your messaging system, you can record them in your MTA and your users need not be bothered by the confusion behind the scenes.
- **Converter:** Program capable of converting from one bodypart format to another. Often, some of the users will be able to process only a limited number of formats (e.g., a VT user will require plain text of some kind and will not be able to use a PowerPoint presentation.) Converters make it possible to convert all the bodyparts from a particular format into another format for those users who require it.
- **Deferred Message:** Message whose delivery has been deferred by the originator until a specified time. Users may not wish for a message to be delivered immediately, but rather at some time in the future. In this case, the MTA can hold the message and pass it on only when it is appropriate. In the meantime, the user may choose to cancel the delivery or allow it to be relayed as scheduled.
- **MPDU:** The various queues hold a number of MPDUs that are being processed by the MTA. It is possible for an MTS manager to examine

these queues and the MPDUs in them in order to diagnose problems with the routing of messages. Quite a wide range of information might be useful in identifying the MPDUs, including originator, recipients, priority, size, state (e.g., "awaiting delivery" or "transfer"), target (agent or next peer MTA), type (message, probe, report), and arrival time.

- **Peer MTA:** Another MTA with a direct (no intermediate MTAs) connection.

  There is a significant difference between MTAs in the same routing domain and those in a different domain: In the same domain they are automatically configured. Since they use the same MTS data, they know about each other implicitly and will establish connections with each other whenever the need arises. If we need to connect a different domain, we will need to manually configure an MTA from our domain to connect to an MTA in the other. Some of the information we may care to configure or look at includes the address of a manually configured MTA, accounting information on the MPDUs transferred (content types, size, priority, originator and recipients and encoded information types); and statistical information, such as the numbers of MPDUs transferred, inbound/outbound connections and inbound/outbound connection failures.

- **Activity:** Transfer of an MPDU from one MTA to a peer. At times it can be useful to examine whether any MPDUs are being relayed between two MTAs. This information on the transfer can be represented by state (e.g., active, idle, interrupted), current MPDU, direction (inbound or outbound) and creation time.

MTS Entity

A message transport system is not an active component. It can be thought of as a collection of MTAs and the data needed to support them. I think it would be beneficial to look again at the MAILbus 400 implementation of MTS routing domains to illustrate how all the components work together.

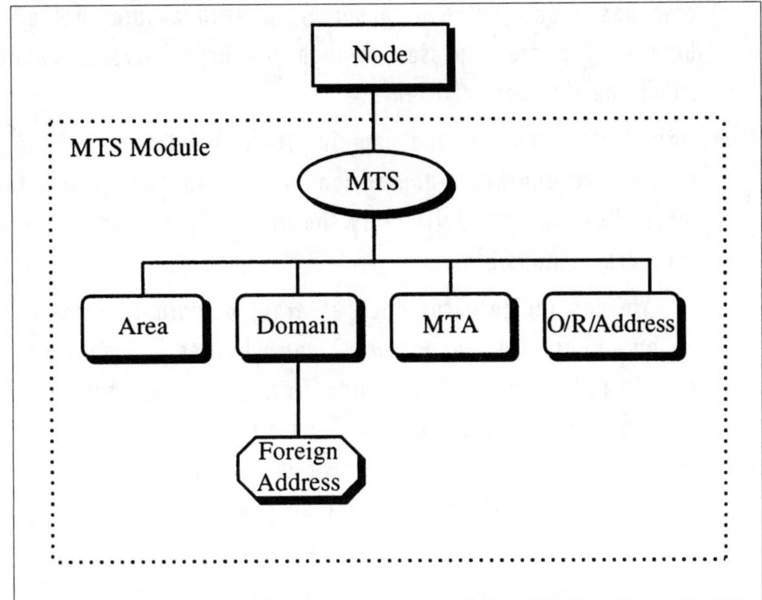

Figure F-3. *The MTS Entity*

The MTS entity does not represent the entire message transport system, but rather a particular routing domain. It is identified by the global domain identifiers (GDIs) that it covers. Figure F-3 shows these objects in terms of MAILbus 400, where they are managed using an EMA director and are called entities.

- **Area:** A group of MTAs, typically in one geographical location. Using Area routing helps to optimize the transfer of MPDUs within a domain. For clarity and elegance it is possible to organize the areas hierarchically.

  For example, without areas we might have MTAs all over the world named MTA1, MTA2, and so on. We could institute areas, one for each city, so that we could address the MTAs as VIENNA.MTA7 and LINZ.MTA32, or SYDNEY.MTA11. With hierarchical routing, we can extend this to AUSTRIA.VIENNA.MTA7, AUSTRIA.LINZ.MTA32 and AUSTRALIA.SYDNEY.MTA11, or even further, to EUROPE.AUSTRIA.VIENNA.MTA7. If each area has a designated area server, we can ensure that all the traffic between the areas passes through the area servers, where the links should be the most efficient.

- **Domain:** Another routing domain. We can define a domain to communicate with another organization, or, via an ADMD, with the world at large. Domains are defined by the global domain identifiers for which they are responsible.

  We can indicate for each external domain whether it is serviced by an agent (i.e., a gateway), or whether its messages should be transferred to another domain (i.e., should go through a specified boundary MTA). In some cases, we may not have a direct connection with a foreign domain. Then we might need to pass the messages through an intermediate, connected domain.

- **Foreign address:** Foreign representation of X.400 address. If a foreign domain is serviced by a gateway (e.g., Message Router or SMTP), the addressing in the domain will not likely adhere to the X.400 conventions. We may be able to address foreign recipients by using X.400's Domain Defined Attributes (DDAs), but they are cumbersome, so a mechanism has been devised to permit a mapping of X.400 addresses to foreign addresses. We can define a mapping for each individual, or we can stipulate a means of converting from an X.400 address to the foreign format.
- **MTA:** All of the MTAs in the MTS must be registered so that automatic configuration is possible when they are needed. Each MTA has a presentation address, and with that any other MTA in the MTS is able to contact it to send MPDUs on.
- **O/R address:** A recipient's address. Usually this is the address of a user, in which case we are able to specify what content information and EITs the user is able to accept. If an MPDU arrives with different content information or EITs, the bodyparts must be converted or the message will be returned to sender. We will also need a routing instruction that indicates one of the following: Redirect (to another O/R address); Transfer to (another server) domain; Nondeliver (the

user is not receiving mail, so a nondelivery report should be issued); Deliver (to a particular agent [user agent, message store or gateway]).

- **Distribution lists:** More commonly handled by the user agents, but can also be registered in the MTS, in which case they simply resolve a distribution list name to a set of member O/R addresses. If required, it is even possible to nest distribution lists, although care should be taken to ensure that there are no recursive definitions.
- **Aliases:** Can be useful if there are alternate spellings (or frequent misspellings) for a person's name, or if someone marries and begins to use a different name. We can define an alias for the old, or less commonly used name, that points to the primary O/R address. When messages come to the alias, it replaces the address and the delivery takes place as expected.

Index